1-19-1989

John Ball —
Keep Mary in
your heart and
your heart will
always be merry!

Mary &
The Power
Of God's Love

Louis Kaczmarek

Louis Kaczmarek

D0150642

TRINITY COMMUNICATIONS
MANASSAS, VIRGINIA 22110

ISBN Paper: 0-937495-29-8
Cloth: 0-937495-30-1

© Trinity Communications 1988

DEDICATION

In grateful thanksgiving to the loving Mother of God, who once saved Her Infant Jesus in a flight for life, and ever since has never ceased trying to save mankind in a flight from sin.

The author and publisher wish to gratefully acknowledge the generous financial assistance of Charles and Helen Bierwirth in the publication and promotion of this book.

Table of Contents

Foreword

Only a few years ago, Louis Kaczmarek gave us the gift of his book, *The Wonders She Performs*. Within 3 years 60,000 copies of it had sold. Now Louis presents to us *Mary and the Power of God's Love*. Again I am privileged to write the foreword to this book by Louis on Our Lady as I was his first.

St. Jerome (d. 420), who wrote the Latin translation of the Bible known as the Vulgate, has often been quoted as saying: "Ignorance of Sacred Scripture is ignorance of Christ." I agree and am also convinced of this: *Ignorance of Mary is ignorance of the Church.*

Devotées of Mary are sometimes wrongly accused of replacing Jesus Christ with Mary. Our devotion to Mary must be balanced. It must be Trinitarian, Christological, Ecclesial and lead to a life of prayer. Solid devotion to Mary must lead to the Father, to the entire Blessed Trinity through the humanity of Jesus Christ. In God's will and providence it is through Mary that we have the humanity of Jesus Christ, our one essential Mediator. "God is one. One is also the mediator between God and men, the man Christ Jesus, who gave himself as a ransom for all" (1 Timothy 2:5).

This book is designed to become available to readers after the Marian year. Pray God that it serve a place in the plan outlined in the encyclical letter of Pope John Paul II, *Mother of the Redeemer.*

Earlier, the Second Vatican Council had presented Mary to us as a perfect model of everything that the Church already is and hopes to become. The Council Fathers did not permit their discussion of the role of Mary to be separated from their consideration of the nature of the Church. Our times have seen a blurring of a proper understanding of the nature of the Church. A renewed Marian interest and a sound appreciation of her role can only help to bring a better and fuller understanding of the Church's nature.

Pope John Paul II brought this out in his encyclical naming the second Marian Year in the Church's history. This was to begin a period of continuous years of preparation with Mary as Model so that we as members of the Church, Christ's Mystical Body, could enter more authentically with Christian faith and love into the beginning of the third millennium of Christianity.

He wrote:

> The Second Vatican Council, by presenting Mary in the mystery of Christ, also finds the path to a deeper understanding of the mystery of the Church. Mary, as the Mother of Christ, *is in a particular way united with the Church,* "which the Lord established as his own body." It is significant that the conciliar text places this truth about the Church as the Body of Christ (according to the teaching of the Pauline Letters) in close proximity to the truth that the Son of God "through the power of the Holy Spirit was born of the Virgin Mary." The reality of the Incarnation finds a sort of extension *in the mystery of the Church—the Body of Christ.* And one cannot think of the reality of the Incarnation without referring to Mary, the Mother of the Incarnate Word.

In his *Mother of the Redeemer* encyclical, Pope John Paul on almost every page keeps reminding us of the faith of Mary which she possessed upon earth. At the same time he adds:

> The pilgrimage of faith no longer belongs to the Mother of the Son of God; glorified at the side of her Son in heaven, Mary has already crossed the threshold between faith and that vision which is "face to face" (1 Cor. 13:12). At the

same time, however, in this eschatological fulfillment, Mary does not cease to be the "Star of the Sea" (Maris Stella) for all those who are still on the journey of faith. If they lift their eyes to her from their earthly existence, they do so because "the Son whom she brought forth is he whom God has placed as the first-born among many brethren" (Rom. 8:29), and also because "in the birth and development" of these brothers and sisters "she cooperates with a maternal love."

This is why I can say, "ignorance of Mary is ignorance of the Church."

God breaks into our time through a Woman. She willingly consented in faith to become the Mother of the Messiah and present the world with its Savior. By the Evangelist writing under the inspiration of the Holy Spirit we know that her blessedness is due not simply to having biologically conceived and given birth to Jesus Christ, but primarily to her faith and response in love. Blessed is she who believed and trusted in the Lord's word, the Scriptures inform us.

Each of us who have been given the gift of devotion to the Mother of God can ask with Elizabeth, "How am I worthy that the Mother of my Lord should come to me?" (Luke 1:43) It is a gift of God to have a deep devotion to Mary. Mary leads us to Jesus in the Spirit as Jesus with the Spirit leads to the Father.

St. Thomas Aquinas reminded us that Jesus, being the Son of God made man, had no faith. Our perfect model in faith then cannot be Jesus Christ who is the object of our faith. The perfect model of faith in the New Covenant must be that Woman which the Bible so clearly presents as the Woman of Faith. Abraham was the man of faith under the Old Covenant. In the New the Woman of Faith becomes the Mother of God and our own spiritual Mother in the order of grace.

Louis Kaczmarek, in this book describing for us the role of Mary in awakening us to the love of God, writes of her who appears in the first pages of Sacred Scripture (Genesis 3:15); who reappears in salvation-history, often not clearly recognized in the pages of the Old and New Testament; and who finally leaps out at us in the last book of the Bible, Revelations 12. There she is seen as the Mother of Jesus and the image of the Church. In an age lacking faith, the world needs desperately to find and renew its devotion to Scripture's Woman of Faith. A world grown cold to love needs this Woman to teach us how to love God and one another in, with, and through Jesus Christ.

I pray that everyone who reads these pages will be brought to a more profound knowledge and love of the Most Blessed Trinity, of Jesus Christ our Lord God and Savior, of the Angels and Saints, of the Church itself. Then, accompanied by prayer, the role of Mary is found in its proper balance.

Father Robert J. Fox
Director, Fatima Family Apostolate

Introduction

With the words of Gabriel's Angelic salutation, "Hail Mary," God sends the most momentous message ever delivered to man, announcing the advent of the Savior of the world and the selection of the Virgin Mary, the humblest of all creatures, to be His Mother. The Eternal Father would entrust Heaven's most precious treasure, His own Divine Son, to Mary, and our salvation would begin!

The magnitude of this profound event is so immeasurable that "all Heaven held its breath" awaiting Our Lady's response. Without Mary's fiat, (be it done to Me according to your word) there would be no New Testament, no Sacraments, no Church, no Christianity, no priesthood, no Holy Sacrifice of the Mass, no Eucharist, no Jesus Christ and no salvation! For these reasons would the early Church joyfully proclaim, "Death through Eve, life through Mary." Devotion to the Mother of God, from then on, would become the hallmark of authentic Catholicism.

Mary's fiat was the first glorious statement that Christ is a universal need. St. John the Evangelist, the Apostle of love, announces this most important fact of history in the simplest words, "The Word was made flesh . . ." (John: 1-14). Mary would become the Divine Mould giving God His Sacred Humanity.

God needed Mary to give Him a body. We need Her to give us a spirit of renunciation and a willing heart to counter the pride that would exalt self at the expense of God, repeating the story of old—Paradise itself.

Oliver W. Holmes said "Mary is half earth and half Heaven." She is more! She is "the missing link" needed in a world gone mad, teeming with confusion and hatred; where the interest in the spiritual is waning while the interest in the flesh is gaining; where social pressures encourage infidelity to God; where 100,000 Moonies would rather follow the Moon than the Son.

In the natural order, there is something abnormal in the physical development of a child that loses its mother in its earliest and most tender years. The same is true in the supernatural order.

> Without Mary our Religion would be psychologically incomplete. The child in us must have a Mother, the man in us must have a lady, and the knight in us must have a queen. In Mary, the child, man, and knight, find their Mother, maid, and queen, their lover and beloved. (Fr. Raymond, O.C.S.O.)

Some years ago, when speaking of the contemporary generation, Fr. Doncoeur said,

> Nourished upon sound doctrine, and the Eucharist, this generation will do much, but it has to discover the Blessed Virgin.

As our 20th century runs its course, with storms raging around us and thunder resounding on the horizon, we are in dire need of Mary's protective function which is essential to Her maternity and to Her reign.

The universally respected Dr. Brownson has stated well:

> I have found it always easy to distinguish those who really love Mary and are really devoted to Her, by their purity of thought and expression. Devotion to Mary marks itself on the features and even in the complexion. We take note, as soon as we see or hear them, that they have been with Mary.

I have spoken of the influence of devotion to Mary in ele-
vating Maternity and with it womanhood. The nations are in
need of this influence still. Christendom is lapsing anew into
heathenism; and the abominations I have referred to as ex-
isting in heathen nations are reviving in nations that profess
to be Christian, and even to a lamentable extent in the bo-
som of nations that call themselves Catholic.

Faith has become weak, and charity has given way to a wa-
tery philanthropy; and the veneration of Mary is branded
idolatry or superstition. Everything is profaned—the Church,
the State, God, Man, and Woman. And Society, while
boasting of its progress, seems to be rapidly lapsing into bar-
barism. Never did the nations more need the Church or the
Pastoral Authority of the Vicar of Christ; never was there a
greater need of the prayers and the intercession of Her
whom we invoke as Health of the Weak, Refuge of Sinners,
Comforter of the Afflicted, and Help of Christians. No small
part of the world, once Christian and adoring the Cross,
needs converting anew.

Efforts to increase devotion to the Blessed Virgin are,
to me, among the most encouraging signs that God has not
forgotten us; that there still are faith and love on the earth,
and that there is still a recuperative principle in Christian society. I thank God, for society itself, that there are still those
who delight to call themselves children of Mary, and do keep
alive in our cold, heartless world the memory of Her virtues,
While She is loved and reverenced, there is hope for society.
And most grateful am I to God that the hard reasonings of
this reasonless age, and the chilling sneers of the proud, the
conceited, the worldly, the corrupt, have not frightened all
out of their deep, ardent and simple devotion to Her who is
BLESSED AMONG WOMEN.

I honor and cherish in my heart of hearts all who honor
Her, and show their devotion to Her by imitating Her
virtues. They are the real philanthropists; they are the real

moral, the true social reformers; and are doing more for society, for the progress of virtue, intelligence, wisdom, than all our statesmen and philosophers put together. They love and honor God in loving and honoring His Mother.

Golden Century

"While Peter has the keys of heaven, Mary has the keys to God's heart; while Peter binds and looses, Mary also binds with the chains of love and looses with the gift of pardon. While Peter is the guardian and the minister of indulgences, Mary is the generous and wise treasurer of God's favor."

(Pope Pius XII: Radio Message, Oct. 12, 1945)

Where is the person to be found who does not enjoy music? It has been called "The universal language", "The speech of Angels", "The language of heaven."

Thanks to the likes of St. Francis of Assisi and his troubadours, and the adventurous laughter of the crusaders, the world reverberated with song and joy in the 13th century. Laughter and song, music and dancing, feasting and health-drinking were prevalent. It was a joyous, spirit-filled time. Religious enthusiasm was the chief inspiration. Romance appeared along with great songs. There was a ferment in the European mind eager to pierce into new fields. Letters awoke with philosophy. The dark ages past, Europe awoke. Universities arose first in Italy, then in Paris. Everywhere Europe was renewed. New white Gothic churches, new castles and new white walls around the cities spoke of a springtime. Never was there the laughter and merriment, love and peace, mixture of nobles and common people as when Mary received Her due veneration as She did in this Golden Century. There was a new spirit of concert and concord as the people contributed to a miraculously quick and magnificent development of the greatest century that the world has ever seen. The whole atmosphere of the 13th century seemed charged with a kind of electricity that sparked the human spirit in a manner that was beyond all earthly precedent.

She who had been endowed with every perfection short of the divinity, had been given Her rightful place. Devotion to Mary reached its peak.

People were reaping the immense benefits having followed Christ's words, "Behold your Mother", and Our Lady's words, "All generations shall call me blessed." Veneration and love of Mary led to God and redounded to His glory. There was never any doubt that Mary led to Christ. Even the newly established devotion, the Rosary, showed that both sides of the beads led one down to Christ on the cross. In his book, the Story of the Rosary, J. G Shaw said of this time,

> In every corner of Christendom, among all ranks of people, there seems to have been a simultaneous outburst of joyous realization that out of all mankind one particular woman had been chosen by God and raised to a position of unique eminence over all the rest of humanity. Priests and people joined in manifestation of honor to this ornament of the human race that they have left succeeding ages—in stone, in all forms of art, in written records, in the liturgy, and in devotional tradition, impressive evidence of a cult of Our Lady which was an unusual combination of broad popularity and tough theological exactness. There arose a strong desire, even the urgent spiritual need, to give expression, to a realization that is bursting upon them—the realization of the beauty, the power, and the glory embodied in that unique work of God, the Woman who conquered Satan and brought Redemption into the world. They see Her as a woman whom God has truly clothed with the sun and crowned with the stars. She stands on the summit of created beauty, reigning alone on the peak of the pyramid of all that is not great and small, to the task of paying due honor to this being set apart from all other beings. They exalt Her

over all other earthly objects of honor, they make Her, once and forever, humanity's Queen of queens.

Of this time, Don Sharkey in his book, *The Woman Shall Conquer*, said,

The people of that time thought of the Blessed Mother in connection with everything they did. They would not venture upon the simplest undertaking without invoking Her aid.

There was a warmth, a compassion, in this century. Even the coldness of displaying the Babe Jesus on an altar by Himself—to show He was the sacrificial Lamb—was changed now depicting His Mother holding the infant in Her arms, or Her kneeling close by looking down upon Him in the crib.

Suddenly Mary became all beautiful, spotless, resplendent as the sun, fascinating, most generous with Her graces. Poetry, architecture, painting, sculpture and music sang of Her glories.

People gave munificent alms; hospitals and churches were built. People led moral and law-abiding lives and worked wonders for the glory of God. Holiness and unworldliness flourished; the clergy were exemplary. Princes were just, people lived at peace with each other and justice and equity reigned.

The cult of Our Lady gave a unique prestige to all architecture. The Eucharist would not be, were it not that Our Lady had housed the Incarnate God. Therefore, every church was an image of Our Lady, and in dedicating a church it was hard to discern whether the formulas were referring to the material building or to Her.

There was a new awareness of Mary and Her role in the Church—and Her likeness to the Church. In this great century, a disciple of St. Bernard, Abbot Isaac of "Stella", a monastery in Poitou, France, brought it out,

> Everything said in the Scriptures universally of the Church,
> Virgin and Mother, is singularly true of Mary . . . The same
> expressions apply to both. Both are mothers, both are vir-
> gins. Both give to God the Father a posterity. Mary fur-
> nishes the Body, its Head; the Church gives this head a
> body. Both are mothers of Christ, but neither gives birth to
> Him completely without the other. (*Dictionary of Mary*,
> Henri Holstein)

She was the first disciple, the first Christian. She is a
"Living Catechism". When She is addressed through the
"Hail Mary", She always responds, "My soul doth magnify
the Lord."

The newly found Orders of this glorious, Golden Cen-
tury, Franciscans, Dominicans and Servites, all promoted
Her veneration: the Franciscans through their seven crown
Rosary, Dominicans with their five decade Rosary, and the
Servites with the five sorrows Rosary. The Carmelites
pushed devotion to Her through the Brown Scapular of Mt.
Carmel. The monastic Orders found in Her the ideal ascetic
and a model for contemplation for She could say, "Thy Will
Be Done', and She could "ponder these things in Her
heart."

Even the English Protestant historian, William Lecky, in
his *History of Rationalism*, spoke of the lofty ideal the
Blessed Virgin Mary gave to Thirteenth Century Europe:

> The world is governed by its ideals, and seldom or never has
> there been one which has exercised a more profound and on
> the whole, a more salutary influence than the medieval con-
> ception of the Virgin. For the first time, woman was ele-
> vated to her rightful position, and the sanctity of weakness
> was recognized as well as the sanctity of sorrow. No longer
> the slave or the toy of man, no longer associated only with
> ideas of degradation and sensuality, woman rose in the per-
> son of the Virgin Mother into a new sphere, and became the

object of reverential homage of which antiquity had no conception.

The moral charm and beauty of female excellence was, for the first time, felt. A new type of character was called into being, a new kind of admiration was fostered. Into a harsh and ignorant and benighted age this ideal type infused a conception of gentleness and of purity, unknown to the proudest generations of the past. In the pages of living tenderness which many a monkish writer has left in honour of his celestial patroness; in the millions who, in many lands, and in many ages, have sought, with no barren desire, to mould their characters into Her image; in those holy maidens, who for the love of Mary have separated themselves from all the glories and pleasures of the world, to seek, in fastings and vigils and humble charity, to render themselves worthy of Her benediction; in the new sense of honour, in the chivalrous respect, in the softening of manners, in the refinement of tastes displayed in all the walks of society—in these, and in many other ways, we detect its influence. All that was best in Europe clustered around it, and it is the origin of many of the purest elements of our civilization.

How consentingly and favorably Our Lady would look upon this prestigious Century for the glorious honor shown Her. She would reward it with Her two greatest sacramentals, the Holy Rosary and the Brown Scapular.

No country was as graced by Our Lady as England. It has been called Our Lady's dowry. The 13th century found a mutual love between Our Lady and England. The bards of England would sing of Her as if their skill were made for nothing else.

As Daniel Sargent wrote in his *Our Lady and Our Civilization*:

By the year 1400 no English poet could count himself a poet

unless he could sing of the Mother of God. Like a medieval craftsman he was no more than an apprentice till he had presented his proper masterpiece, and that had to be in praise of Her. And when he wished to be at his best he had to sing of Her, for the metaphors that had been developed in speaking of Her provided him with his best riches. Thus, Geoffrey Chaucer, whether or not he was feeling pious, but simply when he wished to introduce a highlight into his verse, had the habit of bursting into praise of Our Lady.

The very dress of the English people was not unlike what they would use in a Nativity scene. The Nativity scene had influenced their dress. They were Our Lady's subjects in all their decorum. They saw a flower which they still call "A Lady's Slipper." They saw what we call the "Milky Way" and named it Walsingham Way because it pointed to the Shrine of Our Lady of Walsingham.

They composed special Psalters in honor of Our Lady. The Archbishop of Canterbury, Stephen Langton, would compose one using psalm-for-psalm to correspond with David's. He would call it "A Psalter of Our Blessed Lady." The following is an example taken from that Rosary where the Hail Mary would be recited before each psalm,

> Blessed be the man who walks
> not in the counsels of the impious.
> Hail, Virgin of virgins, Mother without peer
> Worthy to conceive without the seed of man,
> Make us hasten to contemplate
> the law of the Lord
> And to be happy in the glory of Thy Kingdom.

There were a number of such special Psalters. One of the most popular was written by another Archbishop of Canterbury, St. Edmund. In one attributed to St. Bonaventure, Psalter *Immlus Beatae Mariae Virginis*, the first fifty stanzas begin with the word, Ave, the second fifty with Salve, and the third with Gaude. Some authorities see in this a start toward the division of the Rosary into Joyful, Sorrowful and Glorious mysteries.

Of all the provinces that had once been the Roman Empire, Britain was foremost in being enamored of Our Lady's beauty, and was most eager to have Her proclaimed as Immaculately conceived.

William Ware of Warou, teacher of Duns Scotus, began a lecture on Our Lady by declaring, "If I make a mistake in speaking of the blessed Virgin, I prefer that it be in granting Her too much, rather than too little."

The Rosary was promulgated with great rapidity. The expression "Our Lady" was in vogue. "Our Lady's Chapel" could be found in every church. The most common name given to a girl would be Mary. Wayside chapels in Her honour were being erected in great numbers throughout the land.

Alexander of Hales, called the "Irrefutable Doctor" and "The Master of Doctors", had such a strong devotion to Our Lady that it prompted him to make a vow that he would accede to any request made of him in Her name. It was from him that his famous pupils, St. Bonaventure and St. Thomas Aquinas drew their wisdom.

Our Lady would further bless England by appearing to St. Simon Stock at Aylesford and giving him the Brown Scapular of Our Lady of Mt. Carmel. King Edward, with a cheerful heart, would give his opulent castle at Oxford to Our Lady's Order of Carmelites. Nobles would vie with each other in making generous donations to Her shrines. Such was the love Englishmen had for Our Lady. The "Magna Carta", the great charter of English liberties and considered the foundation of modern democracy, was signed June 19, 1215, by King John at Runnymede, securing the liberties of the English church. Individuals now had rights that the Magna Carta was bound to respect. The basic fact that each person is an indestructible creature of God was officially accepted.

With justifiable pride, undoubtedly, would the great English priest, Fr. Faber, write of this time,

> The English Kings were distinguished for their devotion to the Blessed Virgin. They covered their country with those fine Gothic Churches and Cathedrals, which still remain as Her brightest gems of architectural glory. King Edward fasted every Saturday in Her honor, and daily implored Her assistance. Alfred the Great placed himself under Her special protection. Richard the Lion Hearted, built Our Lady of Good Haven before departing for the Crusades—when mortally wounded, and when death was near, he directed in his last will, that his heart should be placed at Our Lady's Shrine.

Historians refer to this period of English history as "Merry old England." Surely this was the case because of Mary. "Keep Mary in your heart and your heart will always be merry!"

In Greece the city of Mystra was known as the hub of intellectual and commercial life, where scholars met and found stimulation and inspiration among each other. Magnificent frescoes cover the walls and cupolas of its six 13th century churches which vied with one another to give the highest reverence to the paintings of Our Blessed Lady found in the Dodekaheortain, the twelve major liturgical feast days of the church year which include the Nativity of the Mother of God, the Entrance of the Mother of God to the Temple, the Annunciation, and the Dormition of the Mother of God.

Scotland would produce the great Duns Scotus who would prove that Mary was indeed the Immaculate Conception—the greatest title She bears next to that of "The Mother of God."

Outside of Cairo, Egypt, is the miraculous shrine of Our

Lady of Damietta, erected in 1220 by Pelagious to counter-act lack of faith in our Blessed Lady, and to atone for blas- phemies directed to Her. To this day miracles have occurred at that Holy Shrine. St. Louis IX, King of France, made it a point to visit the shrine during one of his crusades.

Born in Portugal, St. Anthony of Padua, "The Hammer of Heretics", would proclaim, that with the name, "Mary", he crushed every heresy he encountered. He stated that God does not grant Mary a grace when He hears Her prayers for us, but fulfills an indispensable obligation. He claims, "It is impossible that the Mother of God should not obtain what She asks of Her Son." St. Anthony has been credited with giving us the devotion of praying three Hail Mary's for purity of heart, soul and mind.

St. Elizabeth, Queen of Portugal, was fond of displaying Our Lady's pictures throughout her palace. Her devotion to Our Lady was intense.

The Blessed Virgin Mary frequently appeared to Blessed John Lobedau of west Prussia with Her Divine Child, and conversed with him on the mysteries of Redemp-tion.

St. Simon the Carmelite of Sicily would perform many miracles by simply giving a cup of water to a sick person in the name of Mary.

Russia would proudly give to Our Lady the title of "Empress of all the Russias".

France would build 80 cathedrals and nearly 500 churches in this century. Their great King, Louis IX, was so elated that the word "Jesus" had been inserted after the word "womb" in the Hail Mary, in the year 1251, that he stood daily, praying 50 Hail Mary's, genuflecting every time he came to the name Jesus. He ordered that the Angelus bell be rung at midday to further honor and venerate Mary. St. Louis led several crusades to the Holy Land, bringing back the Crown of Thorns and building the lovely Saint-Chapelle in Paris to receive it. He brought back the first six Carmelites to France from the Holy Land.

The Queen of France, Blanche of Castille, was advised by St. Dominic to say her Rosary every day to ask God for the grace of motherhood. Carrying out this advice faithfully in 1213 she gave birth to her first child, Philip, but the child died in infancy.

Her fervor did not dull because of this disappointment; on the contrary, the Queen sought Our Lady's help more than ever before. She had a large number of Rosaries given out to all members of the court and also to people in surrounding cities of the Kingdom, asking them to join Her in entreating God for a blessing that this time would be complete. In 1215, St. Louis was born—the prince who was to become the glory of France and the model of all Christian Kings.

Far from being insignificant, the Rosary is a priceless treasure which is inspired by God. There is no limit to its power.

The Apostle of the Holy Rosary, Blessed Alan de la Roche, O.P., in his work, *The Importance and Beauty of the Holy Rosary*, tells how Our Blessed Lady gave St. Dominic the Rosary in the year 1214 in a forest near Toulouse, France, after he had prayed for three days and nights, and did penance. She informed him that this was the weapon that the Blessed Trinity wanted to use to reform the world. Comforted and burning with zeal for the conversion of sinners, he crushed the Albigensian heresy with this new weapon from heaven. St. Dominic preached the Holy Rosary for the rest of his life.

Once he preached at Notre Dame in Paris on the feast day of St. John the Evangelist to a congregation made up of theologians and other eminent people used to hearing unusual and polished discourses. St. Dominic told the select group he would not give them a sermon, wise in the eyes of the world, but would explain the Holy Rosary, and began doing so as if he were speaking to little children using simple examples. He began his talk with:

> My Lords and illustrious Doctors of the University, you are accustomed to hearing learned sermons suited to your aesthetic tastes. Now I do not want to speak to you in the scholarly language of human wisdom but, on the contrary, to show you the spirit of God and His Greatness.

Then St. Dominic explained the Rosary as the tool to wipe out sin and to convert sinners and heretics.

Our Lady of Toulouse Shrine was erected in 1212. A statue of Our Lady was placed at the site of a spring where miraculous cures take place. The same statue is there today. Three merchants from Angers were instrumental in erecting the shrine to protect travelers from robbers known to have infested the area.

St. Juliana and Blessed Evelyn, both of Liege, were responsible for the first class Feast of Corpus Christi in honor of the Holy Eucharist.

St. Juliana, in 1209, had a vision, many times repeated, of the full moon in splendor, except for a dark area on one side. She came to understand that the moon represented the Church, and that the dark area was caused by the absence of a feast in honor of the Blessed Sacrament.

In 1254, St. Louis IX gave an ebony image of Mary to the Cathedral of Le Puy, and it has been a place of pilgrimage ever since.

The Dean of the Metropolitan Chapter of Rouen, Richard of St. Laurent, wrote the famous *Mariale Super Missus Est* between 1239 and 1245. It was a remarkable compendium of Marian doctrine and devotion that received wide acclaim. the popularity of this work was enhanced by the fact that it was wrongly attributed to St. Albert the Great.

The Dominicans who came to Ireland in 1224 were remarkable for zeal in spreading love for the Mother of God, which they had inherited from their spiritual father. As early as 1226, in each of their houses, the priests used to go in procession, after Compline, singing the Salve Regina and preceded by a picture or statue of the blessed Virgin. They preached Her privileges; they wrote of Her glories; and with such ardor did they propagate one special form of devotion to Her that, at a much later period in Irish history, they won for themselves the proud title of "The Fathers of the Rosary."

In the second half of the thirteenth century, the tide cast up a piece of wood on the sands opposite the town of Youghal. Because of its rare material, several fishermen tried to take it away; but, though ten horses were harnessed to it, all efforts failed to move it one inch. The receding tide brought it later to a place near the Dominican Convent, founded in 1268, whence two of the friars carried it into the cloister. During the night the prior dreamt that "the image of Our Lady, the Virgin of great power, was in this wood and accordingly it was found in it ." Another account says that while it lay in the courtyard, near the porch of the church, some rain water lodged in its uneven surface. One day, a poor blind man, on his way into the church, dipped his fingers into one of the cavities where the water had lodged. Thinking it was holy water, he washed his eyes in it, and immediately recovered his sight. The incident naturally excited wonder; the beam was carefully cut open, the statue found, and placed in a becoming shrine in the Dominican Church where pilgrims flocked in great numbers.

Their prayers to the Mother of God soon won many favors and even miracles that, after a time, the title of the Church, "Holy Cross" was, with the permission of the Holy See, changed to that of Our Lady of Graces. The shrine continued to be a place of pilgrimage until after the church and friary passed out of the hands of the Dominicans. The little ivory statue, only 3 inches high, was, however, saved. In 1617, the image was enclosed in a case, richly adorned and mounted by a cross with folding doors in front, and returned to the Friars. From that day on it has remained in the possession of the Dominicans, being taken to the Friary in the city of Lee. To this day, no Church of St. Mary is as filled as the Dominican Church of St. Mary. No matter what the weather is, in sweltering heat or cutting snowstorms, each Saturday night, the Church is filled with loving, confident and wholly devoted clients at the shrine of Our Lady of Graces.

Italy would give to the world St. Francis of Assisi, "A giant among saints", "The most Christ-like Saint" who ever lived. St. Francis frequently burst into tears when recalling the great privations to which the blessed Virgin and Her Divine Son were exposed. He once wrote a letter to St. Clare and her community at San Damiano,

> I, your least brother, Francis, will follow the life and poverty of Our Lord Jesus Christ and His Blessed Mother and persevere therein until the end. And I beg and beseech you all to persevere always in this most holy manner of love and poverty.

That his sisters and brothers in Christ might be induced to do this with all the more readiness and spiritual joy, he consecrated himself and his whole Order to Mary, the Mother of God and Mother of the Poor. And the small sanctuary of the Portiuncula, he delightfully called St. Mary of the Angels, which he personally restored at the beginning of his apostolate. There he prayed constantly to Her "that She might vouchsafe to be his advocate." There he rested after his long missionary labors; and there he desired to die, after having commended the place he most loved on earth to the care of his brothers, and chosen Mary as the Patroness of his entire spiritual family until the very end of time.

Thomas of Celano assures us that St. Francis,

> Dedicated to the Mother of Jesus special hymns of praise,
> addressed special prayers to Her, and breathed so many and
> such intimate aspirations of love to Her, that no tongue is
> capable of describing it.

He spent whole nights in praising God and Her; and even
every hour of his Office of the Passion he began as well as
ended with this exquisite antiphon:

> Holy Virgin Mary, there is none like unto Thee born among
> women, daughter and handmaid of the Most High King, the
> Heavenly Father! Mother of our most holy Lord Jesus
> Christ, Spouse of the Holy Ghost, pray for us with St.
> Michael Archangel, and all the virtues of heaven, and all the
> saints, to Thy most holy Son, Our Lord and Master.

Even more exquisite is his "Salutation of the Blessed
Virgin,"

> Most holy Lady, most holy queen, Mother of God, Mary!
> who art ever Virgin, chosen from heaven by the Most Holy
> father! whom He has consecrated with the Most Beloved
> Son and the Spirit, the Paraclete!
>
> In whom was and is all the fullness of grace and all good.
> Hail thou His palace! Hail thou His tabernacle!
> Hail thou His handmaid! Hail thou His garment!
> Hail thou His house! Hail thou His Mother!
> Hail all ye virtues which, by the grace and illumination of
> the Holy Ghost, thou infused into the hearts of the faithful,
> that from infidels ye may make them true to God.

Pope Leo XIII, in his 1879 encyclical, *Aeterni Patris*,
officially confirmed St. Thomas Aquinas as the greatest theologian of the Catholic Church. St. Thomas has been called
"The wisest of the saints and the saintliest of the wise."
From 1265 through 1273 he composed his *Summa The-*

ologica. The book represents reason at its best! A great number of philosophers feel there has never been—and is not likely to be—a single work which better defends Catholic orthodoxy.

He is a great example of devotion to Mary. While still a child, he picked up a bit of paper on which was written the "Hail Mary", pressed it tightly between his hands, then put it into his mouth and swallowed it. His very first words were "Hail Mary", as a child.

As he grew in years, his devotion to Mary became more affectionate and enlightened. Through Her Holy Rosary, St. Thomas sought celestial wisdom daily. He once preached 40 straight days in Rome just on the Hail Mary. In one talk, he claimed there are three things that cannot be improved upon: Heaven, the Humanity of Christ, and Our Lady. I made that statement once in a talk. After the talk, a sallow-faced, stooped shouldered elderly gentleman with a raspy voice questioned me: "Did you say Our Lady could not be improved upon?" "Yes, I did." "Would you please expound on that statement?" Impulsively I responded, "Can you make a perfectly straight line more perfectly straight?" "Can you make a perfectly round circle more perfectly round?" "Mary is perfection personified—how can you improve on Her perfection?" With measured words he thanked me for the explanation.

St. Clare, the foundress of the Poor Clares, and St. Francis' first follower, was called "The foot-step of Mary." Her entire life and ideals were patterned after Our Lady.

Jacapone da Todi wrote the *Laude* dealing with Marian teaching. He composed the Stabat Mater, recited or sung at each of the 14 Stations of the Cross.

Blessed Conrad of Offida was especially devoted to Our Lady with the divine Child in Her arms. He would greet people with, "May the Virgin mild, bless you with Her Holy Child."

St. Margaret of Cortona led a life of sin for 9 years. Comparing her sinful life to Our Lady's life of purity shamed her and was one of the reasons she became a saint.

In 1233, a band of seven young laymen known for their abiding love and devotion to the virgin Mary left their families and successful business affairs in their native city Florence (City of Roses), Italy, to retire outside of the City for a life of poverty and penance. These seven men are known collectively as the seven Holy founders of the Servite Order and were canonized by Pope Leo XIII in 1888. They are Saints, Bonfilius, Bonajunt, Amideus, Manettus, Sostene, Hugh and Alexis. Called together by Mary, they were seven in life, seven after death, and as such have always been collectively invoked.

St. Juliana, O.S.M., founded the Community of Servite Sisters in 1257. The specific mission of the Servite Order is to foster a true and tender devotion to the Mother of Sorrows.

St. Philip Benizi, born August 15, 1223 in Florence, worked many miracles throughout Europe. He was the 5th Superior General of the Servite Order. Down through the centuries after his death, water blessed in honor of St. Philip has been instrumental in effecting remarkable cures.

St. Peregrine, patron saint of cancer patients, was born in Forli, Italy in 1265. In his teens, he was considered a "radical". But thanks to St. Philip, he was converted and became a Servite lay brother.

St. Bonaventure was named by St. Francis. Upon seeing this child who looked like a cherub, he remarked "O Bonaventura"! (from you good things). St. Bonaventure called Mary, "My heart, my soul"! He said,

> She alone has limited the omnipotence of God, who can make a greater earth and a greater world, but cannot make a being greater than the Mother of God.

He was the first to coin the phrase "hyperdulia", which is the veneration given to the Blessed Mother as the most sacred of mortal creatures. "Dulia" is the veneration given to saints and angels. "Latria" is the supreme worship that can be properly given only to God.

St. Bonaventure affirms, "Those who engage in publishing Mary's praises are assured of paradise."

Blessed Peter of Eiena was a simple combmaker. He fostered a special devotion to Our Lady and loved to talk about Her to the customers who came into his shop.

Blessed Angela of Foligno lived only for the world and its vain pleasures. Calling upon the Blessed Virgin to intercede with God for her, she obtained the graces she needed to give up a sinful life—her special devotion was to the Sorrowful Mother Mary.

The custom of dedicating the month of May to Mary originated in Italy in 1280. And the most popular hymns to the Blessed Sacrament, O Salutaris and Tantum Ergo, were composed in that Century by St. Thomas.

Franciscan spirituality, at this time, encouraged devotion to honor the Seven Joys of Mary: Annunciation, Visitation, Birth of Jesus, Adoration of the Magi, Finding of Jesus in the Temple, Resurrection, and the Assumption—normally prayed on the Franciscan Crown Rosary.

The Litany of the Blessed Virgin, also known as the Litany of Loreto, originated at this time. It calls upon Our Lady under 49 titles to pray for us.

1264 saw the Mass for the feast of Corpus Christi composed. In 1269, the first Christmas crib was introduced. In that same year, the Angelus was composed by St. Bonaventure.

In 1294, the Holy House of Loreto was miraculously transported to Loreto, Italy. The house is the very house that was in the town of Nazareth where Mary Herself was conceived. It was the house of the Immaculate Conception, and the Incarnation. No other house in the history of the world has ever been so honored, so sanctified, by what has occurred within its walls—the conception of Mary and the Incarnation of God.

In his book, *The Mother of God*, Father Leonard Feeney said,

> In the year of 1291, at the end of the last crusade, when Jews and Turks were invading the town of Nazareth for the purpose of destroying this holy little house—it was miraculously taken off its foundation and carried through the air to the country of Dalmatia, hundreds of miles away.

Three years later, it was again transported miraculously through the air, carried by angels, and gently deposited in the little town of Loreto, on the northeast coast of Italy.

There is a plaque on the wall, as you enter, that reads,

> Christian pilgrim, you have before your eyes the Holy House of Loreto, venerable throughout the world on account of the divine mysteries accomplished in it and the glorious miracles herein wrought. It was here the most holy Mary, Mother of God, was born, here that She was saluted by the Angel, here that the Eternal Word of God was made flesh.

One of the most striking statements made in the 13th century was by St. Dominic who said, "One day, through the Rosary and the Scapular, She will save the world." Of course the statement has to be qualified. By it he meant that Mary would lead us to Jesus through the sacraments and to a greater love of God and neighbor. In the almost 700 years since the glorious 13th century the only time we see Her with both sacramentals, Rosary and Scapular, is at Fatima, Portugal, October 13, 1917. One may well wonder is that day here?

When the preacher of one of the Crusades, Robert of

Abrissel, had roused the enthusiasm of large numbers of men and women, who were incapable of crusading effort, he united them in the Order of Fontevraul, in which enthusiasm for the Holy Land was replaced by enthusiastic veneration for the Virgin Mary.

"The Knights of the Hospital of St. Mary of Jerusalem", originated in that country to act as ambulance bearers during the Crusades.

During the Mongol invasion of 1241, Poland organized their "Knights of St. Mary" to combat them.

Our Lady of Dusenbach, in 1221, was a celebrated pilgrimage shrine near Ribeauville in Alsace, built by the lord of the place upon his return from the Crusades.

Latvia dedicated their country to Our Lady in 1215 and churches bearing Her name were numerous. The best known shrine is Our Lady of Aglona. In the Buda hills of Hungary, six miles outside of Budapest, is the famous shrine of Mariaremete which flourished with devotion to Our Lady in the 13th century. The chief sanctuary of the Blessed Virgin in Norway, in this golden century, was Her church at Bergen. The Paulist monk, Iskvirin, would be responsible for the shrine to Our Lady of Remete in Yugoslavia by taking this famous statue to the site in the year 1272. Franciscans would establish a house at Locarno, Switzerland in this same century calling it Our Lady of the Rock. Switzerland would build 105 churches in this century all in honor of Mary.

From tradition we learn that in the year 1261, the Lady Richeldis de Faverches was in charge of Walsingham Manor. As a young widow and mother, she had only one desire: "Blessed Mother, show me how best to serve Your Son."

Our Lady appeared and asked: "Will you build a duplicate of the Holy Family home in Nazareth? This home will honor the joy of the Annunciation and it will be a place of prayer for all." When it was built Richeldis led her household to the little Holy House.

Adolph of Schaumburg, Germany, was blessed when Our Lady appeared to him on his deathbed and told him a great reward was his in heaven. He had always displayed a tremendous love for Mary.

St. Albert Magnus, The Universal Doctor, tutor of St. Thomas Aquinas, preached Our Lady's powerful intercession. "She is to be asked, for if She is asked, it will be done," and "Next to being God, comes that of being the Mother of God; and She could not be more united to God without becoming God," were some of his famous statements. He loved to call Her "Mother of the Church" and "The Treasurer of Jesus Christ."

Germany would enrich the church with two famous Benedictines, Saints Gertrude and Mechtilde. St. Mechtilde's desire was to compose a prayer in honor of God's Mother greater than any previously composed. Our Lady spoke to her and told her, "Desist from your labor, for no prayer you could possibly make would give me more joy and delight than the Hail Mary."

St. Gertrude celebrated all of Our Lady's feasts with a joyful heart and expected special favors from Her on these days. On the vigil of the Feast of the Assumption of Our Lady, she asked Our Lord to obtain for her the good will of His sweet Mother, as she feared she had never been sufficiently devout to Her. St. Gertrude delighted in praising Mary as "paradise of delight" and "most beautiful habitation of God." She implored Our Lady to fill her heart with virtues so that God would take pleasure in dwelling therein.

What is the history of Poland without Mary? In a letter, *Gloriosam Reginam*, to the Polish Bishops, dated December 8, 1955, Pope Pius XII stated,

> For a long, long time the people of Poland, with a devotion difficult to equal, have honored and venerated the glorious Queen ... In return for Her devoted children's testimony of

their homage, that Mother of god and of men, whose bounty
matches Her power, has granted graces generously to that
people . . .

Our Lady blessed Poland because of its great devotion
to her in the thirteenth century by seeing that Her famous
icon, "the Black Madonna", was brought by Prince Ladislaus
Opolczyk from Belz, western Ukraine, and enshrined in
Czestochowa on August 26, 1382. Originally, the famed icon,
attributed to St. Luke, was brought from Constantinople by
Princess Anna, wife of St. Vladimir, grand-prince of Kiev, to
the Ukraine in the year 988.

While I toured Poland in 1978, I asked a number of religious, at Czestochowa, why they thought Our Lady would
have wanted Her famed icon to come to Poland? Almost all
replied because of the tremendous devotion the Polish people have *always* shown to the Mother of God.

The Polish people had such a marvellous respect for the
name of Mary that it was centuries before they would name
their girls with Her sacred name.

The King of Spain, St. Ferdinand III, honored Mary
under Her title, "Help of Christians", with great confidence.
He had Her image carried at the head of his troops as their
standard. He converted the great mosque in the re-con-
quered city of Cordova into a beautiful church and dedicated it to the Mother of God while battling the Mo-
hammedans.

King Alfonso X, in 1284, was the first to associate Mary
with the month of May in his songs (Cantigas) of Mary.

St. Peter Nolasco, when still a young man, went from
France to Spain and gave away his great wealth to ransom
Christians enslaved by the Turks. He even expressed a strong
desire to be sold himself to replace those poor slaves.

One night, while he was considering this idea, the
Madonna appeared to him, Her face most serene. She told

him that She and Her Son would be most pleased if an Order were founded with the special mission of freeing Christians enslaved by the Turks. It was to be called "Our Lady of Mercy".

St. Peter went to his confessor, Saint Raymond of Penafort. On that very night the Blessed Virgin had also appeared to St. Raymond and expressed the same desire to him. While the two men of God were conferring, King James of Aragon arrived. The Madonna had also appeared to him that night and had told him to help the Order that She wished founded in Her honor.

August 10, 1218, the three men started the new religious Order and named it after Our Lady.

The royal dynasty of Hungary gave the Church Blessed Cunegunda and St. Elizabeth. As an infant, Cunegunda was heard to say distinctly, "Hail, Queen of Heaven, Mother of the King of Angels!" When she was carried to church, she kept her eyes raised to heaven during the holy sacrifice of the Mass and would bow her little head whenever she heard the holy names of Jesus and Mary.

St. Elizabeth, the patron saint of 3rd Order Franciscans along with St. Louis IX, was Cunegunda's aunt. St. Elizabeth became "holy in a hurry" practicing imitation of Our Lady's virtues.

Frederick A. Harkins, S.J., in his "Mary's Meaning For The Individual" states,

> What the Blessed Virgin Mary has been able to accomplish in a bygone era for the cultural flowering of men and society is a matter of record. It all but constitutes a history of Christian civilization. Faith and free devotion were the doors that admitted Mary to the inviolable world of human wills, and there She worked Her wonders.

Able, because She was invited, to bring sanctity to souls, to humanize and ennoble character, to soften and purify manners, to evoke what is most chivalric in hearts, to consecrate natural beauties and kindle warmth in human relations, to arouse the finest outburst of Christian valor, to inspire the most luminous triumphs of Christian art, Mary, with Her gentle compelling presence, was once so influential that even a studious non-believer like Henry Adams could call Her, "the greatest force the western world ever felt."

Mary's Importance

"It has been allowed to the august Virgin to be the most powerful Mediatrix and Advocate of the whole world with Her Divine Son."
(St. Pius X: *Ad Diem Illum*, Feb. 2, 1904)

One of the most important tasks of Vatican II was to set devotion to Mary within the context and heart of the Church. In so doing, the Council Fathers sought to strengthen devotion to Mary. This devotion was to lead to imitating Mary as a disciple of Jesus, to live by His love, to serve His people, to be part of His suffering, as St. Paul says, ". . . to fill up what is lacking to the Body of Christ."

The Council Fathers, of course, hoped that we would heed Her requests at Fatima when She asked for prayer, penance, reparation. She in turn said Russia would be converted and we would have an era of peace in the world.

Why then, has Russia not been converted after all these years? Why is there no peace? What has gone awry with the message of Fatima? Unfortunately, there are some who have misunderstood the Council and have backed away from devotion to Mary. Devotion to the Mother of God has been down-graded in general. It is no wonder then, that devotion to the Lady of Fatima, specifically, should suffer. Scarcely 2% of the people in the world know about Fatima and the peace plan Our Lady offers us.

Today, it appears chic to de-emphasize Our Lady's role in the Church. Bishop Fulton J. Sheen said, "If you hear someone praising Our Lady today, it'll more than likely be a Protestant. If you hear someone putting Her down, it'll be a Catholic."

There are those who would have us believe Mary no longer commands the power, authority, respect, importance and attention She once did command. They are wolves in sheep's clothing. For God bestowed more grace upon Mary in Her Immaculate Conception, than He did upon all the Angels and Saints combined.

To find out how much power this Lady commands, go to the authority of authorities—to God Himself. Listen to what God says to Satan about Her power in the Bible's first book, Genesis 3:15. Incidentally, it is the first sermon ever preached—by God Himself—to Satan about Her power!

> I will put enmity between you and the Woman, between your seed and Her seed; She shall crush your head, and you shall lie in wait for Her heel. (Gen 3:15)

With the exception of God Himself, have you ever heard of power like that?

If you want to know how much authority this Lady commands, realize this. God created Her to be the Mother of God. She would contain in Her womb Him whom the entire universe could not contain! With the exception of God Himself, have you ever heard of authority like that?

If you want to know how much respect She commands, open up the Bible to the first chapter of St. Luke, the 48th verse, and read Our Lady's own words, "Henceforth, all generations shall call me blessed; because He who is mighty has done great things to me." With the exception of God, have you ever heard of respect like that?

Christ, being God, could say, "Learn of Me for I am meek and humble of heart." This was a proof of His Divinity, for what man who ever lived could publicly say those words without being a laughing stock? By the same token, what woman who ever lived could say, "All generations shall call me blessed," and not become a laughing stock except a Mother of God?

If you want to know how much importance She commands, realize this. The Third Person of the Blessed Trinity, the Holy Spirit, made Her the first and the most beautiful of all tabernacles—a living tabernacle! She would contain in Her womb, Jesus Christ—Body, Blood, Soul and Divinity—for the first nine months of His earthly sojourn. The Second Person of the Blessed Trinity, Jesus Christ, made Her the Mother of the Church. The First Person of the Blessed Trinity, God the Father, made Her the Queen of Heaven! With the exception of God Himself, have you ever heard of importance like that?

If you want to know how much attention She commands, realize this: Jesus Christ spent three hours on the cross redeeming all mankind; 3 years establishing and instructing His Church, and 30 years giving His attention to Her!

Although it is true that Our Lady could never celebrate the Holy Sacrifice of the Mass, nor could She ever consecrate the Sacred Species, but more truly than any ordained priest could She look upon the bleeding body of Her Son as He hung on the cross at Calvary, and literally say, "This is My body!" "This is My Blood!"

Consider, too, that She is the Daughter of God the Father! She is the Mother of Jesus Christ the Son! And She is the Bride of the Holy Spirit!

Our Lord Himself said, "By their fruits you will know them" (Matthew 7:20). That being the case, what more need be said of Mary—Christ is the Fruit of Her womb!

Our day finds people craving the gifts of the Holy Spirit. St. Louis de Montfort said,

> When the Holy Spirit finds Mary in a soul, He enters that soul completely and communicates Himself completely to that soul.

Of course, this means with His 12 Fruits, 7 Gifts, 4 Cardinal Virtues and 3 Theological Virtues.

Belgium's Cardinal Suenens reiterated this when he said, "Where Mary is, that's where the Holy Spirit is!"

Bishop Fulton J. Sheen said, "Our Lady is the only person who looked down on Heaven—when She held the Christ-Child in Her arms."

Holy Mother the Church has had thirty-two Doctors of the Church. They are the greatest theologians the Catholic church ever produced, by its own declaration and admission. It seems it is more difficult to be a Doctor of the Church than to become a Pope. We have had 263 Popes and only 32 Doctors. To be a Doctor of the Church, three things are required: eminent learning, holiness, and you must have expounded upon some truth of Catholicism or defended it. And it seems as though there is a fourth qualification—you must have a burning love for the Mother of God, because you cannot name one Doctor who was not on fire with the love of Mary.

St. Anselm has been called "The Doctor of Mary." He said of Our Lady's power: "Whatever God can do through His infinite power, Mary can do the same thing through Her prayers." And He also said,

> It is impossible that a devotee of Mary who faithfully pays homage to Her and recommends his soul to Her be damned. This applies to true devotees, who wish to amend their lives, not to those who make abuse of this devotion to sin more.

St. Alphonsus de Liguori is so highly regarded by Holy Mother the Church that he has been proclaimed the patron

Saint of all the Doctors, the patron Saint of all moral theologians, the patron Saint of all confessors, and the patron Saint of all vocations; and he is the Founder of the Redemptorists. He said God would refuse Mary nothing, and that, "A true child of Mary will never be lost."

St. Thomas Aquinas, the Angelic Doctor, the wisest of the saints and the saintliest of the wise, said,

> It was very reasonable that the Lord should distinguish the Queen from the servants, His Spouse and His Mother from His vassals. The great dignity of Mother of God, to which she was chosen and elevated, is an order of hierarchy superior to all that is purely created, and which approaches more nearly the limits of the Divinity.

St. Bonaventure, the Seraphic Doctor, said,

> It is the privilege of the glory of Mary, that after God, our greatest happiness is from Her.

St. Augustine, the Doctor of Grace, states,

> If all the tongues of men were put together, and even if each of their members was changed into a tongue, they would not suffice to praise Her as much as She deserves.

St. Bernard, the Mellifluous Doctor, composed the magnificent *Memorare*:

> Remember, O most gracious Virgin Mary, that NEVER was it known, that ANYONE who fled to thy protection, implored thy help or sought thy intercession, was left unaided. Inspired by this confidence, I fly unto thee, O Virgin of virgins, my Mother; to thee do I come, before thee I stand, sinful and sorrowful. O Mother of the Word Incarnate, despise not my petitions but in thy mercy hear and answer me. Amen.

St. Albert Magnus, The Universal Doctor:

She knows all, and is ignorant of nothing. In the first instant, She was more instructed, more learned, more intelligent, and wise, in every kind of art or science, as well natural as supernatural, human as Divine, than not only all the wise and learned men of the earth, but even the angels and most sublime spirits of paradise.

St. Robert Bellarmine, Model of Defenders of the Faith:

And who would ever dare to snatch these children from the arms of Mary when they have taken refuge there. What power of hell or what temptation can overcome them if they place their confidence in the patronage of this great Mother, the Mother of God, and of them?

St. Peter Damian:

As the light of the sun so greatly surpasses the light of the stars that in it they are no longer visible, it so overwhelms them that they are as if they were not; so does the great Virgin Mother surpass in sanctity the whole court of Heaven.

St. Catherine of Siena is one of two lady Doctors of the Church. She said,

Mary is a most sweet bait, chosen, prepared, and ordained by God to catch the hearts of men.

St. Teresa of Avila, the other lady Doctor, said,

The devotions we practice in honor of the glorious Virgin Mary, however trifling they may be, are very pleasing to Her Divine Son, and He rewards them with eternal glory.

Anyone who turns to Mary will never be disappointed.

Even though the love of Mary rejects and abhors anything contrary to honesty and morality, She will always be more willing to help us than we are to beseech Her help, no matter how sinful we are.

Bishop Sheen often told the story of how, one day, Our Lord was going through Heaven and observed undesirable people there. He approached some of the Angels and Saints asking, "How did all of these people get into Heaven?" "Don't ask us Lord. You gave St. Peter the keys to the Kingdom of Heaven, ask him." Our Lord approached St. Peter and repeated the question. St. Peter replied, "Don't blame me Lord. I kept the doors locked, but Your Mother kept opening the windows!"

In a church in Texas I met the priest who had written this story for the *Catholic Digest*. An indigent family lived not far from the Church. They had a little boy, age 4 to 5 years, who pleaded with his mother for a new red wagon for his birthday. She told him to pray to the Infant of Prague—the Baby Jesus, a statue of which was in the church. The boy prayed every day begging for the wagon. His birthday came. No red wagon! "Why, Mommy?" "Don't ask me, Son, you go and ask the Baby Jesus."

The priest was in the sacristy when he heard the door of the church open. He peeked out and observed the little boy walking down the center aisle. Pitter-patter were the sounds his little shoes made as he approached the statue of the Infant of Prague. With tears streaming down his cheeks, his lips trembling, the boy said quite loudly, "Jesus, I'm gonna tell Your Mother on you!"

Mary is gentle and kind to all who have recourse to Her. What can be more encouraging than the thought that we have a Heavenly Mother who is powerful and in whom we can take refuge, while asking Her to grant all that we need for our well being and salvation.

Even after he had left the Catholic Church, Martin

Luther wrote in his *Die Erklanung des Magnificat*, in 1521,

> The great thing about Mary is none other than She became
> the Mother of God; in which process so many and such
> great gifts are bestowed upon Her that no one is able to
> comprehend them.

Thereupon follows all honor, all blessedness and the fact
that in the whole race of men, only one person is above all
the rest, one to whom no one else is equal. For that reason
Her dignity is summed up in one phrase when we call Her
the Mother of God. No one can say greater things of Her or
to Her, even if he had as many tongues as leaves and blades
of grass, as the stars of heaven and the sands of the seashore.
It should also be meditated in the heart what that means, to
be the Mother of God.

In what assuredly was the only legislative resolution of
its kind in the history of the United States, the Illinois Senate, on Sept. 8th, 1985, voted to honor the 2,000th anniver-
sary of Our Lady's Birth (Sept. 8th). The resolution, which
was sponsored by Senator Richard Kelly, read:

> Whereas, motherhood reached its highest plateau when
> Mary, the Virgin, was chosen to be the Mother of Jesus
> Christ, . . . this is the appropriate time to recognize Mary on
> the occasion of Her 2,000th Birthday anniversary.

The measure also called for the Governor, James R.
Thompson, to declare December 8th, the Feast of the Im-
maculate Conception, "as the date to honor Mary, the
Blessed Virgin." (St. Louis Post-Dispatch, Dec. 1, 1985).

When the First World War was at its height, Pope
Benedict XV, on May 5, 1917, made a vehement appeal to
the Catholic World for a crusade of prayer to Mary for
peace, in these words:

From every corner of the earth—from the majestic churches and the humble chapels, from the mansions of the rich as well as from the huts of the poor, from wherever dwells a faithful soul, from the bloodstained battlefields and war swept seas, may this pious and ardent invocation arise to Mary, the Mother of Mercy, who is all-powerful in grace!

Seventy years later Pope John Paul II announces a "Marian Year" in his homily for the Feast of Mary, the Mother of God on January 1st. Addressing Our Blessed Lady, he said:

The Church fixes her eyes on you as her own model. She fixes them on you in a special way in this period in which she is preparing to celebrate the coming of the third millennium of the Christian era. In order to prepare herself more worthily for this special event, the Church turns her eyes to you, who became the providential instrument whom the Son of God used to become man and to begin these new times.

For this intention she desires to celebrate a special year dedicated to you, a Marian Year which, beginning this coming Pentecost, will end the following year, with the great Feast of Your Assumption. It will be a year in which every diocese will celebrate with their own initiatives, for the purpose of deepening your mystery and favoring devotion to You in a renewed commitment of conformity to the Will of God according to the example offered by You, the Handmaid of the Lord.

His encyclical, "Mother of the Redeemer" calling forth the Marian Year, says it is a hopeful sign that Catholics and other Christian churches are reaching an agreement on fundamental points of Christian belief, including matters related to the Virgin Mary.

The following proclamation was issued by the Mayor of St. Louis, Missouri:

OFFICE OF THE MAYOR
CITY OF SAINT LOUIS
PROCLAMATION

WHEREAS St. Louis will be privileged to host the visit of the renowned International Pilgrim Virgin Statue of Our Lady of Fatima from June 2 - June 26, 1987; and

Whereas, this Statue has been the instrument of many marvels in many parts of the world; and

Whereas, Pope Pius XII blessed and crowned this rosewood likeness in 1947 for the purpose of travelling throughout the world on a mission of peace; and

Whereas, it is hoped that through this visit to St. Louis of the Queen of Peace many people will follow the requests of Our Lady for prayer and penance so the reign of peace will be granted to mankind as promised by Her at Fatima, Portugal in 1917, and many are gathering in respect and appreciation of this important symbol of Faith.

Now, therefore, I, Vincent C. Schoemehl, Jr., Mayor of the City of Saint Louis, do hereby proclaim the Month of June 1987, as

INTERNATIONAL PILGRIM VIRGIN MONTH

in St. Louis.

The love that all Mothers have had for their children is but a shadow in comparison with the love that Mary bears to each one of us. She loves each one of us more than all the Angels and Saints put together. She is easily found by those who seek Her. How easy it is for those who love Mary to find Her, and to find Her full of compassion and love.

"Go to this Mother of Mercy," says St. Bernard, encouraging sinners, "And show Her the wounds which thy sins have left on thy soul; then will She certainly entreat Her Son, by the breasts that gave Him suck, to pardon thee all. And this Divine Son, who loves Her so tenderly, will most certainly grant Her petition."

St. Alphonsus Liguori said,

> When devotion to Mary begins in a soul it produces the same effect that the birth of this Most Holy Virgin produced in the world. It puts an end to the night of sin and leads the soul into the path of virtue.

St. Germanus supports St. Alphonsus's statement,

> To pronounce the name of Mary with affection is a sign of life in the soul, or at least that life will soon return there.

Eagerly would St. Bernard proclaim, "All generations shall call me blessed." "Because She has begotten life and glory for all generations of men."

Our Blessed Lady revealed to St. Bridget that,

> there is no sinner in the world, however much he may be at enmity with God, who does not return to Him and recover His grace, if he has recourse to Her and asks Her assistance.

Saint Blosius said,

> There is not in the world any sinner, however revolting and wicked, who is despised or rejected by Mary; she can, She wills, and She knows how to reconcile him to Her most beloved Son, if only He will seek Her assistance.

No wonder the famous English author, J. Ruskin, said,

> I am persuaded that the veneration of the Madonna has been one of the noblest and most vital graces of Catholicism, and has never been otherwise than productive of true holiness of life and purity of character.

And St. Ephrem said:

> Don't you know that Mary is the hope of those who are despairing, of those of whom one despairs, of those of whom one should despair?

Our model for our relationship with God is Jesus. Our model for our relationship with Jesus is Mary, who has been extolled as the model and inspiration for all walks of life, for all vocations, for all Christians.

The Founder of Graymoor, Fr. Paul, a convert to Catholicism from Anglicanism, found it inconceivable for any Christian who professed love for Jesus to deny loving His Mother. He said, "there is no lie forged in hell more in conflict with the word of God expressed in Scripture and Catholic Tradition, than the Protestant conceit that they honor Christ best who most ignore the existence of His Mother."

Abbot Arnold of Chartres remarks,

> Since the flesh of Mary was not different from that of Jesus, how can the royal dignity of the Son be denied to the Mother?

The God of Life became Her Son!

Our Blessed Mother is most anxious for us to repent so that we can be with Jesus and Her forever in Heaven. There Jesus will be our greatest joy. Mary, our second greatest joy. the stunning fragrance of Her presence will perfume Heaven with its titillating aroma and augment the joy of all inhabitants. Looking upon Her dazzling beauty and hearing Her golden-toned, dulcet voice will call to mind the stirring Biblical words, "No eye has seen, nor ear heard, nor the heart of man conceived what God has prepared for those who love Him."

Our Immaculate Mary's charm, grace and elegance will

excite admiration unquenchable. Little wonder, then, St. Peter Damian would say,

> The greatest glory of the blessed in heaven is, after seeing
> God, the presence of this most beautiful Queen.

Little wonder too St. Bonaventure would say,

> After God, our greatest glory and our greatest joy is Mary.
> As a mirror broken into a billion fragments, and each one
> reflecting the sun, so each soul will be lost in Her captivating
> beauty. Her golden gaze will melt everyone.

No artist or poet has ever captured Her resplendent beauty,
but for all eternity will the chambers of heaven echo forth a
chorus of praise from billions of souls, "Hail Mary"—only to
hear Her sonorous reply, "My Soul doth magnify the Lord."

Our Immaculate Mother deserves our honor. She is the
stairway to Jesus. She is the ideal of every living soul. Mary is
God's greatest creation and Queen by Divine Appointment.
Jesus gave Mary to us that She might Mother us. Therefore,
if we want to enter the Kingdom of Heaven directly, let us
love, honor and imitate our Immaculate Mother. She will
recognize us after death, if we wear Her Brown Scapular
during our lifetime.

Monsignor Ronald Knox said this of Our Blessed Mary,
"she is more than a theological symbol. she is to each one of
us a personal romance."

Even when Knox was still an Anglican he kept a faithful
vow never to preach a sermon without at least one reference
to Mary. Shortly before he died in 1957, he wrote,

> Other lights may grow dim as the centuries pass, but Mary
> will never suffer change. When a Catholic ceases to honor
> Mary as Virgin and Mother of God, they will cease to be a
> Catholic.

O Mary, You are the Cornerstone of the Eternal Design! Here is the *Te Deum* of St. Bonaventure to the Mother of God.

TE MATREM LAUDAMUS

We praise Thee, O Mother of God: we acknowledge Thee
    to be the Virgin Mary.
All the earth acknowledges Thee as the only Daughter of
    the Father.
All the Angels and Saints serve Thee.
The Powers and all the Dominations obey Thee.
The Cherubim and Seraphim praise Thee, crying
Holy, Holy, Mary Mother of God and pure Virgin
heaven and earth are filled with Thy glorious majesty.
The glorious Choir of the Apostles praise Thee.
The admirable Company of the Prophets praise Thee.
The white-robed army of Martyrs praise Thee.
The whole army of Confessors praise Thee.
The Holy church in all the world acknowledges Thee,
Thou Empress of infinite Majesty and
Worthy Mother of God's only son.
Also Immaculate Spouse of the Holy Spirit.
Thou, O most Holy Virgin, art a Queen of honor.
Thou art the chosen Daughter of the Eternal Father.
In order that man may be saved, Thou hast conceived
the Son of God in thy womb.
By thee, the old serpent was crushed, and Heaven
was opened to the faithful.
thou dost sit at the right hand of Thy son in the
glory of the Father.
thou art believed to be the reconciler of the future Judge . . .
Therefore, O Mary, we pray Thee
to come to the assistance of Thy servants,
Whom Thy son has redeemed with His Precious Blood.
Make them to be numbered with Thy saints.
in glory everlasting . . .
O, Mary, save Thy clients and bless them
who honor Thee,
Govern them; and lift them up forever.
Day by day, O Mary, keep us from mortal sin.
O Mary, take pity of us; please take pity on us.

Show Thy mercy to us as we have hoped in Thee.
O Mary, in thee have I hoped,
may I never be confounded. Amen.

Most people belong to some club or organization. So let us, Her Marian sons and daughters, join Our Lady's Army as She marches on to crush the power of Satan. Let us be Her crusaders to save souls, to snatch them from the devil.

Our Immaculate Queen is our Commander. Her Banner is the Cross of Christ Her Son. As we follow Her, Her loyal subjects and slaves, our weapon is the Holy Rosary! Our distinctive uniform must be Sanctifying Grace and our distinguishing insignia is the Brown Scapular. Seeing our Brown Scapular, one will know we are sworn to allegiance to Our Blessed Mary. Our marching song is—IMMACULATE MARY—our Battle hymn is—HAIL HOLY QUEEN—our BATTLE CRY at every moment is the HAIL MARY . . . Our motto—To Jesus Through Mary!

When a day comes that we feel tired in this struggle against the powers of darkness, let us immediately remind ourselves that Mary's beautiful eyes are upon us and She is smiling and thanking us for the love and sacrifice we are putting forth. We cannot fail Her or disappoint Her. Her happiness and Her smile mean everything to us.

We can face the infernal enemy with Our Lady at our side to protect us. We will do all She asks and repeat often, "Totus Tuus" (I am All Yours)!

Let us attend the Holy Sacrifice of the Mass often (daily if possible), our nourishment being the Holy Eucharist. This will give us the power to fulfill our daily duties lovingly and conscientiously.

The following is from St. Louis de Montfort,

But the power of Mary over all the devils will especially shine forth in the latter times, when Satan will lay his snares against Her heel; that is to say, Her humble slaves and Her

poor children whom She will raise up to make war against
him. They shall be little and poor in the world's esteem, and
abased before all, like the heel trodden underfoot and per-
secuted as the heel is by the other members of the body. But
in return for this, they shall be rich in the grace of God,
which Mary shall distribute to them abundantly.

Mary, Mediatrix of all graces! This title teaches us that
Mary is the Dispenser and the Channel of grace as it comes
from the Father to His Son, Jesus, and from Jesus to Mary
and from Mary to each person. Mary, being in Heaven, sees
what graces we need. And being our Mother, She worries
about us and cares deeply that we do not lose our souls. Let
us all unite in praying that Our Holy Father will proclaim
with a Papal pronouncement that: *Mary Is The Mediatrix of
All Graces!* to all the world, of all faiths and races. Whether
they know Her or not, whether they are aware of Her
mediation or not, She nevertheless disposes of all favors and
graces from the Father and the Son.

In Bethlehem when shepherds and countless visitors
came to see the beautiful, newborn Baby Jesus they must
have asked,"what is this lovely Mother's name?" Mary gave
Jesus the first kiss, the first smile, the first embrace. She was
the first to do all the precious, loving, tender things that only
a mother can do for her child. Mary must have sung the first
lullaby to Jesus with Her sweet voice, and how Jesus must
have loved and cherished each thing His Beloved Mother
did for Him. The joy of joys is—that She is our Mother too.
She is just as tender and solicitous towards us, especially if
we call on Her and say, O Mother Mary, please be my sweet
Mother too! I need you so very much. Please help me and
take care of me. How could She refuse? Never will Our
Lady, the Mother of God, refuse us. Instead, She will
immediately run to our side to help us in each need. She
loves us that much. Try Her! And see what happens!

The late Cardinal Mercier established a Feast in honor

of Our Lady Mediatrix of All Graces, and he also composed the Office for it. He also worked towards the solemn definition of this doctrine. He begged Pope Benedict XV to pronounce as Catholic Dogma the traditional belief of Christian people in the universal intercessory Mediation of Mary. The Pope did appoint a commission to prepare and to obtain the solemn definition, but so far, it has not been defined.

The words of St. Ephrem are appropriate here:

> My Lady, most Holy Mother of God, full of grace, inexhaustible abyss of God's unseen gifts and largesses, the channel of all graces, next to the Holy Trinity Mistress of all things, after the Paraclete a second Consoler, and after the Mediator the Mediatrix for the whole world, behold my faith and my desire given me by God. Do not despise my unworthiness, nor let the malice of my actions impede Thy immense mercy. O Mother of God, O name most delightful to me! There is no securer trophy than Thy help.

A noted theologian wrote:

> Among the members of the Mystical Body, she holds a special place of Her own, the first after the Head. In the Divine organism of the whole Christ, Mary performs a function which is intimately bound up with the life of the entire body. She is its HEART ...

The Heart always symbolizes love, but when a heart is wounded or pierced, it symbolizes suffering love. We see this suffering love in the Sacred Hearts of Jesus and Mary. St. Pius X wrote:

> Prescinding from our charity toward God, who can contemplate the Immaculate Virgin without feeling moved to fulfill that precept which Christ called peculiarly His own, namely, that of loving one another as He loves us?

The Apostle John writes: "And being with Child, She cried, travailing in birth." John saw the most Holy Mother of God in eternal happiness, yet travailing in a mysterious childbirth. What birth was it? Surely it was the birth of us who, still in exile, are yet to be generated to the perfect charity of God, and to eternal happiness. This shows the love and desire the Virgin from Heaven above watches over us, and strives with unwearied prayer to bring about the completion of the elect.

St. Archelaus referred to Mary as "The most chaste Virgin and Immaculate Church."

Auguste Nicholas explained this about Mary:

> If the Church is like Mary, Mary is the living form of the Church. And it is through Her that God pours into the Church, life and fecundity—the Church is thus, so to say, the expansion of the maternity of Mary—it is the mystical womb of Mary, which gives birth to the Mystical body of Christ.

St. Paschal Baylon's two great loves were the Blessed Sacrament and the Blessed Mother. He died during the consecration of the Mass on Pentecost, May 17, 1592. God allowed a miracle to occur during his funeral service. During the consecration of the Mass, at the elevation, Paschal Baylon's eyes opened and closed as if in adoration.

St. Paschal frequently said this: "Man should have the heart of a child toward God, the heart of a Mother toward his neighbor, but toward himself the heart of a judge."

As a young Jesuit, St. John Berchmans made a vow always to defend the Immaculate Conception. Our Blessed Lady inspired him to do that.

Because of his lifelong love for Mary, St. Robert Bellarmine was ready to die. When he was told his end was near, he said three times, "O good news!" Our Lady came to escort him Home.

Juan Diego, a poor Indian of Mexico, to whom Our Lady appeared on a little hill of Tepeyac in the year 1531, was always childlike in His conversations with Mary. On one occasion when he was worried that his uncle might die without a priest, he took another route in order not to meet Our Lady. She, however, came down from the top of the hill toward him. Our Lady asked him if he were worried, and he explained all of his anxieties to Her. After listening patiently to him, She said:

> Listen and understand well my son, smallest of all, that you have no cause to be frightened and worried. Let your heart be troubled no longer, have no fear of sickness or any other sorrow. Am I not your Mother here next to you? Are you not here in the shelter of my loving shadow? Am I not your health? Are you not safe here within my loving bosom? What else hast thou need of? Let NOTHING worry or afflict you further.

When Juan Diego heard this from Blessed Mother, he ceased worrying. We can apply these beautiful words to our life. They are meant for us too.

Our Lady also told Juan Diego, "I am a Merciful Mother to all who love Me and trust Me, and invoke My help."

Père Lamy was an old French chaplain who died in 1931. He frequently saw Our Blessed Mother and talked with Her. He said She was always surrounded by a thousand Angels. She would call each Angel by name most lovingly but they always praised Her as Queen. Mary is, Queen of the Angels and Queen of Heaven and Earth.

Pope Pius XII wrote:

> As vast as Jesus' dominion is, nothing is excluded from Mary . . . she rules Purgatory and Hell's demons are powerless against Her. They expect God to be able to vanquish them but it galls Satan that a mere creature by the graces She can procure for her clients, has enabled them to reach the goal of heavenly joy, and a vision of God.

God is Love

"The Mother of God, minister of heavenly graces, was placed at the zenith of power and of glory in heaven to give the help of Her patronage to men searching their way on earth among many fatigues and dangers."
(Pope Pius XII, *Sollemne Semper*, Aug. 15, 1932)

This gentle Woman comes marching into our 20th century undaunted by deaf ear, indifference and opposition. Like a dove winging its way with unquestioning love, She comes asking us to love God, to love our neighbor. Would that we had an eraser to wipe away the painful hurt caused Her by our refusals.

Throughout the long record of the developments of poetry, sculpture, painting and music, Her beauty, clothed in the rays of His Divinity, has stimulated ever higher and more perfect achievements,

> As the innocent moon, that nothing does but shine,
> Moves all the labouring surges of the world.

Father Albert Power, S. J., M.A., in his book *Our Lady's Titles* says,

> Our Lady's influence on the world has ever been a refining, elevating, ennobling one. She has lightened the load of millions, has brought peace and joy to tortured hearts, counsel to those in doubt, comfort to the sorrowing, repentance to sinners, and the love of God to cold and listless souls. What

59

a work for God She has been since She came into being!

Our Lady will teach us the self-sacrificing effort to understand others, to let them come alive as persons worthy of respect simply because they are persons, created by God, redeemed by Christ, spiritually begotten by the Blessed Mother. The Blessed Mother can heal modern man by restoring him to true friendship with his neighbor. Today's society would have us look at our neighbor as a "thing", which may be useful or harmful to our own advancement.

In silence and solitude She searches souls in a voice most articulate for Her Son.

Gently She whispers not to yield to our natural desires, but follow the promptings of grace. We can change the course of life by a kind word or a generous deed; by our example we can lead souls either to heaven or to hell.

With Her Son, She would tell us ever so gently,

> No man can serve two masters. For either he will hate the one and love the other, or he will sustain the one and despise the other. You cannot serve God and mammon. (Matt. 6:24).

It is especially by teaching a man to sanctify his daily work that the Blessed Mother will restore in large measure the lost sense of human worth.

Our Blessed Mother is the Mother of Jesus. Jesus is our Brother. Mary, therefore, is our Mother. She is the Mother of all mankind: the atheist, the agnostic, the deist, the pantheist, the pagan, the Jew, the Protestant and the Catholic. She loves us so ardently, that St. John Bosco said if you take all of the love of all of the mothers who ever lived, and place it on one side of a scale, and place Our Lady's love, just for you, on the other side of the scale, Her love for you will outweigh all of the love of all the mothers who ever lived!

She would have died on the cross—just for you—in place of Christ. But that couldn't be, because a God-man had to die for our sins.

The Statue of Liberty holds the torch of freedom, while Our Lady holds the light of the World, Christ, Her Son! Her message for all mankind is, and always has been, an echo of Her words to the waiters at Cana, "Do whatever He tells you." That is absolutely the greatest piece of spiritual advice Planet Earth has ever received! In essence, Our Lady tells us at Fatima: I don't want you to have ill will toward anyone, I don't want you to gossip, slander, back-bite, detract; I don't want you to hurt, to hate, to kill. Rather, She would have us pardon, respect and love everyone.

Mary has a consuming desire to win souls from sin to holiness, from creatures to the Creator, from the things of time to those of eternity! She wants to people Heaven!

Thomas Merton in The Seven Story Mountain says:

> Mother of God, how often have you not come down to us, speaking to us in our mountains, and groves and hills, and telling us what was to come upon us, and we have not heard you. How long shall we continue to be dead to your voice and run our heads into the jaws of the hell that abhors us?

Over 1900 years ago, Our Lord walked this earth. One day He was approached by a Pharisee who was a lawyer, and was asked this question, "Master, which is the greatest of all the Commandments?" Our Lord answered, "You shall love the Lord Your God with all of your heart, with all of your soul, with all of your strength, and with all of your will." What is thought-provoking is that the Pharisee asked for but one Commandment—the greatest! But Our Lord gave him two. And He said, "The second is like unto it, you shall love your neighbor as yourself."

That is precisely what Fatima is all about, the love of God, and the love of neighbor. Before Our Lady came to Fatima, an angel appeared to the three children, Jacinta, Lucia, and Francisco in his first of three apparitions that would take place in 1916.

It was the spring of the year when the budding woods were beautified with birches, junipers and chestnuts. The terrain was rolling and hilly. A light breeze stirred. There was a restless awareness about the children as the angel gently knelt on the soft ground, and addressed himself as the Angel of Peace. He spoke in a voice of middle range. He had a noble way of speaking, clipped, clear, concise. The children were wide-eyed as the angel taught them to pray this prayer which he repeated three times:

> My God, I believe, I adore, I hope, and I love you. Forgive those who do not believe, do not adore, do not hope, and do not love you.

A perfect prayer encompassing both the love of God and the love of neighbor.

In the summer, on a day when the wheat fields gleamed in the slanting light of a brilliant sun, and a few dark clouds rolled low in the distance, almost with breathless impatience, the angel addressed the children:

> Pray! Pray a great deal! The Hearts of Jesus and Mary have merciful designs for you! Offer up prayers and sacrifices to the Most High as an act of reparation for sin which offends Him, and for the conversion of sinners. But, above all, accept and bear with submission all the sufferings Our Lord will send into your lives.

In the fall, under a gray sky, on an oppressive day, unseasonably cool, and a moist gust of wind, the angel came for the last time. He held a glistening, gold chalice in his left hand. Above the chalice, in his right hand, he held a consecrated Host. Drops of blood were falling from the Host into the chalice. Leaving both suspended in the air, the angel prostrated himself upon the ground and taught the children to pray this prayer which he prayed three times,

> Most Holy Trinity, Father, Son, Holy Spirit, I adore Thee profoundly, and I offer Thee the Most Precious Body, Blood, Soul, and Divinity of Jesus Christ, present in all of the Tabernacles throughout the world, in reparation for the outrages, sacrileges and indifferences by which He is offended. Through the infinite merits of the Sacred Heart of Jesus and the Immaculate Heart of Mary, I beg for the conversion of poor sinners.

The angel then arose, and holding the chalice and the Host again, he gave the Host to Lucia, and the contents of the chalice to Jacinta and Francisco, while he said,

> Receive the Body and Blood of Jesus Christ, so horribly outraged by ungrateful man. Console your God and make reparation.

That terminated the apparitions of the Angel of Peace. In the first apparition, he placed the emphasis on prayer; in the second, on penance; in the third, on reparation; thus laying the ground work for Our Lady who would come a year later on May 13, 1917, in Her first of six apparitions to the same children asking the same things: prayer, penance, reparation.

In 1946 Mr. William Thomas Walsh, who wrote perhaps the most popular book on Fatima, interviewed Lucia, the sole survivor of the children, and he posed this question to her, "Lucia, what kind of penance do Jesus and Mary want from us?" One wonders if, when asking that pertinent question, Mr. Walsh might not have envisioned the wearing of hair-shirts, denying ourselves food, sleep, drink—punishing our bodies. Lucia promptly, affably, answered that the penance Jesus and Mary want from us, at this time, is to see God's Will in all of the activities of our daily, normal lives—especially those things we do not like that we cannot change. Remember what the angel said in his second apparition . . . "Above all, accept and bear with submission all the sufferings Our Lord will send into your lives."

Send them He will. Christ Himself told us, "If you would follow me, deny yourself, take up your cross and follow me." Our Lord is telling each and everyone of us—in no uncertain terms—that we all have a cross to carry in life. It cannot be escaped! But, when He sends these crosses, we are to love God with all of our heart, with all of our soul, with all of our strength, with all of our will, and to love our neighbors as ourselves!

Pope Paul VI said that the greatest need in the world is to truly love our neighbor. The real Christ-like, Marian test of love of neighbor, if we should want to check ourselves, is what we think of our neighbor. Human nature being what it is, the tongue will often reveal what the heart contains, thus causing quarrels and wars. Sometimes people have wondered how much they love God. The Saints have answered that question: We love God no more, no less, than we love our neighbor.

One of the most beautiful passages in Sacred Scriptures is the 25th chapter, the 31st verse of St. Matthew:

> Come you blessed into the Kingdom of Heaven, for when I was hungry, you gave me to eat; when I was thirsty, you gave me to drink; when I was naked, you clothed me; when I was sick, you took care of me; when I was in prison, you visited me; when I was a stranger, you took me in.

You can read between the lines. When I so urgently needed that telephone conversation to lift my failing spirit, you took the time to phone me. When I needed that letter to inspire me to persevere, you took the time to write it. When I needed that pat on the back to see me through my daily trials and tribulations, you were always there with words of encouragement. When I needed that Christ-like smile, you gave it to me every day. When I needed that loan to see my family through, you gave it to me. When I was a Lebanese hostage, you prayed for my release. When I was confused and in need of advice, you listened and counseled me.

Lord, when did we see you hungry, thirsty, naked, in prison, sick, confused, a stranger? What follows are some of the most awesome words ever spoken: "Amen, amen, I say to you, as long as you did it to one of these, the least of my brethren, you did it to me."

A 9th century Persian poet penned these immortal lines,

> I sought my soul, but my soul I could not see. I sought my God, but my God eluded me. I sought my neighbor, and there, I found all three.

Perhaps that is why Christ, before He left this earth, said, "A new Commandment I give you, that you love one another. By this will ALL people know that you are my followers."

There is a poem that is haunting,

> I shall pass through this world but one time. Therefore, any good that I can do, or any kindness that I can show, let me do it now. Let me not defer it nor neglect it, for I shall not pass this way again.

When an uncle of mine passed away, my father paid him a beautiful compliment that has stuck with me ever since: "I never heard him say an unkind word about anyone." What a lovely way to be remembered!

St. John of God, a great lay saint of Spain, said,

> Do all the good you can, to all the people that you can, in all the ways that you can, at all the times that you can, in all the places that you can, as long as you can.

And his contemporary, the great St. John of the Cross,

a doctor of mystical theology, said,

> In the twilight of our lives, God will judge us on how we loved.

St. Joseph Benedict Labré said,

> Do you want to be happy and holy? Then you must have three hearts in one:
> 1. A heart of fire for the love of God.
> 2. A heart of flesh for your neighbor.
> 3. A heart of bronze for yourself.

St. Francis of Assisi said,

> Lord, make me an instrument of your peace. Where there is hatred, let me sow love; where there is injury, pardon; where there is doubt, faith; where there is despair, hope; where there is darkness, light; where there is sadness, joy.

> O Divine Master, grant that I may not so much seek to be consoled as to console; to be understood as to understand; to be loved as to love; for it is in giving that we receive, it is in pardoning that we are pardoned, and it is in dying that we are born to eternal life.

One of the most beautiful, but one of the saddest, love stories I have ever come upon took place in a city in Michigan. A wife asked her husband to watch their 5-1/2 year old boy while she went Christmas shopping. She said she would be gone for two hours. She was gone for five. Quite naturally, the boy acted up. The father was short on patience. He grabbed a broom, with the handle, proceeded to beat the boy unconscious. After he realized what he had done, he grabbed a blanket, wrapped his boy's body into it and dashed out to his car as fast as he could with his son in his arms. He drove to a nearby hospital. Picking his son up into his arms, running up the steps of the hospital, the movement jarred his son back into consciousness. Opening his eyes, with tears streaming down his cheeks, his lips trembling, he said to his father, "Daddy, I still love you." Within one hour, he was dead.

That was Christ speaking through that little boy, through the Mystical Body. He tells that to each and everyone of us no matter how many times we offend Him by sin—"I still love you!"

What is love? St. Paul tells us in his 1st Corinthians, 13th Chapter,

> Love is patient, love is kind, love envies no one. Love is never boastful, nor conceited, nor rude, nor selfish, nor quick to take offense. Love keeps no score of wrongs, does not gloat over other men's sins, but delights in the truth.
> There is nothing love cannot face. There is no limit to its faith, its hope, its endurance.

Love is the greatest virtue of all. God is love! Sometimes a Mother will ask her child, "How much do you love Mommy?" while extending her hands away from each other indicating with her fingers the amount of love. Christ loved us with arms parallel to the ground, extended in opposite directions as far as they would go—nailed to the cross, shedding His blood for our salvation.

That in its simplistic form is the message of Fatima: the love of God, the love of neighbor, through prayer, penance, reparation.

Since God is ALL Love, we his poor human creatures must return to Him as much as is possible for us to give. Once we fall in love with God we must try and nurture that love throughout our lifetime. Jesus is always willing to strengthen and deepen our love for Him if we come to Him and ask Him. Jesus says to us: "Come to Me all you who labor and are burdened and I will refresh you." Our dear Lord knows very well that we are wounded by original sin, but with our love, prayer and everyday effort, each day we can begin anew on the road to perfect love of God.

If we practice this perfect love of God as far as we are able, then even on this earth we will reach spiritual maturity (which includes, as Our Lady of Fatima asked, sacrificing ourselves for sinners) and this spiritual maturity will help us understand our role in the work of Redemption. We will have strength and receive it from Holy Communion, because Holy Communion gives us the energy and the graces necessary to help Jesus save souls, in union with Him.

It may enter into our mind that if God is all love why does he allow evil? Well, we must believe that evil would not be allowed by God if He could not get good from it. God allows an evil to obtain a particular result. Let us accept conditions as they are, all the while praying, working, sacrificing for the transformation of souls and society.

In this great work of transformation we have Our Immaculate Mother and Queen who is our leader in our work of co-redemption. We learn from Our Blessed Mother that when we suffer for others, Jesus suffers in us. We live and die for Jesus. We belong completely to Him, as we unite our trials and sufferings with His Cross, for the salvation of countless souls, and for our own conversion.

We live in difficult and trying times, but we can become strong souls if we are faithful to adoring Jesus in the Holy Eucharist believing in His real presence, if we are faithful to and follow the Holy Father as he upholds Catholic doctrine, and if we are faithful to Mary, our Mother and Queen.

Sister Faustina Kowalska, of the Sisters of Our Lady of Mercy, is called the Apostle of Divine Mercy. Our Lord made known to her how much sin there is in the world. Seeing all this horrible sin, she asked Our dear Lord, "Jesus, why do you not punish and annihilate all these sinners?" Jesus answered, "Because my dear daughter I have all eternity for my vengeance! During the sinners' lifetime I want to pour out all my Mercy upon them."

Our Lord told us, "Without Me you can do nothing." This means that God gives us the graces for whatever He asks us to do. All the work is done by Him, what we add is our own free will. We, who have been redeemed by Jesus and are His adopted children, have the total assurance of His Love forever. This truth should give us great security and peace of soul. The Truth of God's total love for us should spur us on to do His Will at every moment of our busy day. We will then be willing to accept whatever happens in our life, and we will accept lovingly whatever God sends into our life.

God's love for us is true love. And what is true love? True love is sacrifice! As we look at the crucifix, we see true love giving every drop of His Precious Blood so that each human being on the face of this earth could be saved and have eternal happiness with that Loving God.

If we claim to love someone yet we cannot sacrifice ourselves for that person, it is not true love. Christ is our model. Let us gaze upon Him daily and ask Him to teach us to love as He did.

St. Anthony Mary Claret wrote,

The man who burns with the fire of Divine Love is a son of the Immaculate Heart of Mary, and wherever he goes, he enkindles that flame. Nothing deters him: he rejoices in poverty; he labors strenuously; he welcomes hardships; he laughs off false accusations; he rejoices in anguish. He thinks only of how he might follow Jesus Christ and imitate Him. He cares only for the glory of God and the salvation of souls.

St. Paul of the Cross wrote in a letter:

Love is a unifying virtue which takes upon itself the torments of its beloved Lord. It is a fire reaching through to the inmost soul. It transforms the lover into the one loved. More deeply, love intermingles with grief, and grief with love, and a certain blending of love and grief occurs. . . .

Therefore, be constant in practicing every virtue, especially in imitating the patience of our dear Jesus, for this is the summit of pure love. Conceal yourselves in Jesus crucified, and hope for nothing except that all men be thoroughly converted to His Will.

God is our all—our truest and best Friend. We are recipients of His care and providence. Every new day is His precious gift to us. Another day to love Him and praise Him with our entire being. To love God is not only our joy but it is also our duty. We have only one heart to give, so let us give it to the God of love who created it in the first place.

May Our Immaculate Mary lead us to Jesus and teach us to know and love Him as She Herself knew and loved Him!

"God forbid that I should glory, save in the Cross of Our Lord Jesus Christ" (St. Paul, *Galatians*).

God's infinite love has only one aim, to save every individual, and bring each person to His eternal Home to enjoy unending happiness. We, therefore, must help God and Our Blessed Mother in saving sinners. Bishop Sheen said, "Every soul has a price tag on it." We can help save souls best if we accept our suffering and crosses, and unite them with the Cross of Jesus, as expiation for their sins. The saints who are now in Heaven understood thoroughly this wisdom of suffering and assisting Jesus in saving souls.

In today's ultra-modern lifestyle, material things are coveted with great eagerness. Yet, we must meditate on this transitory life, and know in our heart and mind that God alone is our destiny and our coveted dream. When we swerve from this path God allows us to undergo some type of suffering to bring us back to the true reality of Himself and eternity.

Let us speak to Jesus perhaps in these or similar words:

My Sweet, Beloved Jesus, please use me as your humble assistant (helper) in saving souls, many sinners, from eternal damnation. I will do my best to accept lovingly all the crosses, trials and sufferings you send to me. May my reward be only YOU and Your IMMACULATE MOTHER as we rejoice with You and all the souls we rescued from the disaster of Hell. Amen.

If we live in this manner and assist Jesus in this fashion, perhaps we may bypass Purgatory and be ushered into Heaven immediately after death. God is never outdone in generosity! Jesus once said to St. Rose of Lima, "Rose of my Heart, you take care of My interests, (saving souls, etc.) and I will take care of your interests." Jesus is true to His word.

God calls us with His love! How many times we have offended our good God again and again and merited eternal punishment. But then Jesus forgave us instantly in His sacrament of Reconciliation. What a great joy and consolation to be a Catholic and to be able to confess our sins to Christ in the person of a priest! God is constantly showering us with favors and surprises great and small, throughout the day and throughout our lifetime. Let us take the time to reflect on them and thank God for His benevolence. God could have created thousands of other people but instead He thought of us and created us to love Him, and serve Him with all our hearts. Let us love God to folly, since we can never love Him enough. All eternity will not be enough to love our God! And let us always remember that FEELINGS do not count. Love is in the Will. We may not feel that we are loving God, we may feel dry and indifferent, but as long as we *will* to love God and praise Him, it is most acceptable to God and more meritorious than if we were filled with sweet, emotional feelings. It is true love in action, in practice. Husbands and wives likewise do not always feel romantic love toward each other, nevertheless, their love is real and true and they will to love each other till death do them part.

Love is in the will. Feelings come and go depending on our moods and other circumstances.

Our Lady is our perfect model. She loved God unceasingly. That is why God found Her irresistible. She waited for God's Will and fulfilled it humbly, thanking Him and praising Him all the while.

St. Augustine prayed:

> My God, and My Life and sacred delight. What can anyone say when he speaks to God? yet woe to them who are silent about him. When even those who say most are but dumb.

St. Francis of Assisi loved Jesus more passionately than other Saints. He once said, "My brethren, let us begin today to REALLY love Jesus Christ."

Father Faber wrote: "If every night we would ask the Blessed Virgin to offer to God the Precious Blood of Her Son, that thereby one mortal sin, which would be committed that night, would be prevented, think what sorrow to Jesus would be forestalled." Every soul is important in the eyes of God. No one is forgotten by God, although they may be repulsed by humans.

It is a greater task to bring a sinner back to God than to create another world. We should be willing to pay any price and make any sacrifice to save sinners from losing their souls for all eternity. When we receive Holy Communion we may beg Our Lord to save sinners, many of them that day. If we accompany these requests with fervent prayer and the sacrifices of our daily duty, Jesus will answer our request for souls. We will discover how many souls we have saved after our own death, when it will be revealed how many people arrived in Heaven due to our prayers. What happiness we will experience at the sight of all the souls we helped save.

Let us love the unlovable in our city and town. They are more in need perhaps than others of our help, our smile and our prayers. Nothing really matters in the end, but that we remain in the grace of God and help others place themselves in God's grace. If we never lose God's grace, we have a permanent union with God. We have the adorable Blessed Trinity dwelling in us. Let us guard that Life fiercely. Even if we lose our parents, our health, our mind, our best friend, it is all only temporary, someday sooner than we think we will have eternal happiness in heaven. All that was taken away, we will have in abundance in eternity in the presence of Almighty God, His Holy Mother and all the Angels and Saints!

Jesus, meek and humble of heart, make our hearts like unto Thine.

Jesus always chooses humble, honest, hardworking people to do His work. He loves the lowly ones. God Himself chose Mary, who was unknown, humble and unassuming. St. Joseph falls in the same category, and so with thousands of Saints in the past and in the present, as we look at our present Holy Father, Pope John Paul II, Mother Teresa, Father Patrick Peyton, Mother Angelica, and to many others who are hidden except to the eyes of God.

Of course, we have reason to be humble. Everything we have is a gift from God. All we possess are our many sins.

With humility comes ease in obedience. Being obedient to God's Will has its rewards. We can tell God that, since we are doing His Will, He must arrange that all works out perfectly for us! And if we have the patience to wait, it does work out beautifully! When we look back over the past years of our life, and see how we blindly set out to do God's bidding, it all turned out marvelously well, and now we wonder why we ever worried in the first place. God is the Master of all, and He takes care of those who love and trust Him. Let us learn to be submissive to the inspirations from on High, and be keen to look for the sign language of heaven as to what we are to do or not do.

Great accomplishments mean nothing to God He looks

at our heart and how much we love Him, which is the purpose of our existence on this earth.

Our present Holy Father said this in Boston: "Follow Christ, you who are married, share your burdens with each other and Him." And in New York City he said: "When you wonder about your role in the future of this world, in the future of your country—look to Christ. Only in Him will you fulfill your potential as a citizen of America and the world."

Hail Mary

"She is our kindest Mother, who has shown Herself always, in the face of every danger, our powerful helper and channel of grace."
(Pope Pius XII: *Auspicia Quadam*, May 1, 1948)

Kneeling at my bedside as a child, I first heard the lovely words, "Hail Mary," from my mother. Her warm, gentle, loving hands would take my small right hand and trace the Sign of the Cross upon my head and shoulders to be followed immediately with "Hail Mary, full of grace . . . " This would be the order of the day before I could jump into bed.

"Boys and girls, quiet please. And stay in your seats!" I was in a strange world: school! Soon I was learning I had a Guardian Angel. I learned about Jesus. I was surprised to learn I had another Mother who had the same name as mine. Sister Anastasia told us this Mother was our heavenly Mother. She sees us. She loves us. She is the kindest Mother God ever created. She wants us, someday, in Heaven with Jesus and Her. We made our Heavenly Mother happy when we obeyed Jesus. We made Her happy when we prayed the "Hail Mary."

In the 2nd, 3rd and 4th grades, Sisters Alphonse, Stanislaus and Clemens, respectively, would accentuate the importance of praying the Hail Mary. Each one would relate exciting stories about the Hail Mary that were impressionable in our young minds.

While in the 5th grade, I was delighted upon hearing

the story, from an adult, who was an avid Notre Dame football fan, how in one game, Notre Dame was in need of a touch-down. Into the huddle, a Hail Mary was prayed. The next play resulted in a touchdown pass which tied the game. Upon receiving the ball again, and going into a huddle, the quarterback was indecisive and asked for suggestions. Immediately the only Protestant on the team blurted out, "Let's pull that Hail Mary play again!"

Report cards today! Father Mayotte would be invited to give us the cards. He would scrutinize every mark with a deep interest. He made you feel important. He was most sympathetic, most encouraging. He always culminated the event by way of a little talk. This day he emphasized how pleased Jesus is when we go to Him through His Mother, just as any father is pleased when his child goes to him through the mother. Smiling, he said, "When you want something badly, something inside of you says, go to Mom!"

The lunch bell was ringing. My pockets bulged with the marbles I had just won as I scampered to Sister Berchman's 6th grade class. She always taught the importance of punctuality. There was a spark, a vitality, about her that made you want to please her. With the greatest joy and enthusiasm she introduced us to St. Thérèse, the Little Flower, and taught us to pray frequently when in need, "Little Flower, in this hour, exert your power." I liked St. Thérèse! I especially liked her upon finding out she never performed any action without first having prayed to Our Lady. And how I was amused to hear the story how she was once asked, "Thérèse, do you pray to the saints?" "No, I never pray to the saints. They take too long to answer. I pray to Our Lady—She answers immediately."

I was so sold on Our Lady, the Hail Mary and the Rosary by this time, that when it was announced our art class was to have a contest, I drew a picture of a nun presenting a Rosary to a person, convinced I should take first place because of my subject. Second place was my reward.

Four years of high school saw to it we all stood at 12:00 noon and prayed the Angelus in honor of Our Lady. I loved it because it contained three Hail Mary's.

Before I was out of high school, my father started a family business—today it is a corporation—with a picture of Our Lady, 50 cents, and a Hail Mary. The picture had been brought from Poland by my grandmother. That picture, today, hangs in a most prominent place of honor in the plant.

In our neighborhood lived a charming old lady, Julia Havens, whom everyone fondly referred to as "Granny". She was spry, lighthearted. She had a good word for everyone, and was loved by all. I attended school with her grandson, Don. Proudly, Don would display a picture of Granny when she was a glamor queen, 18 years of age, winning the contest for "Miss Bay City."

Now in her seventies, her one jet-black hair was silver; her once smooth, peach colored, face was wrinkled and ashen gray.

Often Don and I would spend hours listening to her enchanting tales of old Ireland. She always sat in a rocker with a blanket on her lap and a rosary in her hands as she excited us with folk story after folk story.

One fine day I took Granny a flower and told her I was going into the military service. "Always be good." "Don't drink." "Stay away from bad company." "Always pray the Rosary daily." These were her words of admonition to me. Somewhat apprehensive about the uncertain future, I asked, "Granny, would you please pray for me while I am away?" "I promise you I will pray the Rosary for you every day!" Thomas-like, I actually doubted that she would keep such a promise.

Each furlough I found time for a quick visit to see Granny, always taking her a box of candy or a flower in grateful appreciation for that daily Rosary which I valued tremendously. Inevitably—as though she could deduce my suspicions—she always confirmed her promise before I would bid adieu.

Years later—my tour of duty completed—I was preparing for bed one bitterly cold, January night. My night prayers said, a quick glance at the clock—10:45 p.m.—a snap of the light switch, I hopped into bed. Suddenly the most peaceful sensation coupled with a mesmerizing aroma enveloped me. It was uncanny! Within seconds I felt the presence—very powerfully—of Granny in my darkened room! It was comparable to a foretaste of heaven, I felt! Somehow, someway, it was communicated to me, spiritually, that Granny had prayed a Rosary for me, faithfully every day while I was in the service!

A heavy pounding on the door early the next morning roused me out of bed. Anxiously waiting to come out of the cold was my friend, Don. Quickly the coffee was on. Don was very glum. "What is wrong Don?" "Granny died last night." After a quick shudder of shock, I asked "What time?" "10:45 p.m."

While I was in the U. S. Air Force, the Korean war waged hot and heavy. Matt Talbot, the holy man of Dublin, came influentially, irresistibly into my life at this time. I was enthralled absorbing with great zest, page after page, Eddie Doherty's *Matt Talbot*. This unlettered man, having fallen to the lowest dregs through alcoholism—hitting the pits—rose up to the highest heights of sanctity. On page 48:

> For Matt Talbot was a contemplative, one whose soul continually turned towards God, one whose mind was absorbed in God. . . . Though only a humble laborer far removed from the influence of conventual discipline, the record of his austerities bears comparison with the best of saintly anchorite or monk of old. Perhaps we could go further and say that, considering the circumstances of his life, it eclipses, in all likelihood, most penitential records of the past.

Rapt in wonder, I pondered how would this man have attained such tremendous grace. Matt himself answered the question, "No matter how drunk I was, I never failed to say one Hail Mary to Our Lady every day. She obtained the grace of conversion for me!" Of course, it was Our Lady! "She is our kindest Mother, who has shown Herself always, in the face of danger, our powerful helper and channel of grace." It is Our Lady's delight to exercise Her powerful influence with God in obtaining for us whatever graces we need.

I had no difficulty in accepting Matt's answer. The brilliant Spanish Jesuit, Francisco Suarez, shortly before he died, said he would gladly give all the many learned books he wrote, and all his life's labors, for the merit of one Hail Mary! As St. Bernardine of Sienna said,

> Mary gives to whom She wills, the way She wills, when She wills, and as much as She wills, the graces of the Eternal Father, the virtues of Jesus Christ, and the gifts of the Holy Spirit.

The Korean War was at its peak. My brother-in-law was inducted into the U.S. Marines. A long-awaited furlough, just in time for Christmas, was my lot. My sister, Virginia, said her husband would be home from the service to celebrate the holidays with us. Though I would not in any way discourage her, I was convinced, beyond a shadow of a doubt, his chances were a big goose egg, nil, zilch! "Do you really feel Bert will be allowed to come home for Christmas, Virgie?" "I am praying this 30-day Rosary to Our Lady, it is unfailing. He will be home!"

The day she completed the 30th rosary—one day before Christmas—she received a telephone call. Her weary husband had traveled most of the day and a good portion of the evening. Arriving at the depot, we found him sound asleep, exhausted from travel and anticipation. This event left a tremendous impact on my. I've never forgotten Virginia's deep faith in the Lady of the Rosary, nor Our Lady's response.

My furlough completed, I returned to Chanute Air Force Base, Rantoul, Illinois. My work in the Orderly Room, as a Career Guidance Specialist, granted me ample opportunity to canvass all incoming literature destined for our office. One fine summer day, a Chicago Tribune newspaper carried a gruesome story, and picture—the aftermath—of a fiery collision, in Chicago, between a huge gasoline tanker-truck and a bus filled to capacity. One woman on the bus escaped the ordeal. Forty-six perished in flames!

In an interview she told reporters, upon impact, the entire bus was engulfed with gasoline and flames. Amid shrieks of terror, a stampede for the exits ensued. It was a race against death! She was near the back door, helpless, frozen with fear and horror. Two powerful men, panic-stricken, pounded ferociously, futilely on the door. Flames cloaked the door. The intense heat quickly claimed their lives. They dropped, lifeless, at her feet. Realizing she was but one breath from death, filled with reverential fear, she desperately cried out, "Holy Mary, Mother of God, help me!" Immediately the door opened! As soon as she stepped out, unscathed, the door mysteriously closed! She was the lone survivor.

At the time it was difficult to know what struck me most: 46 people ushered into eternity—when they least expect it; or, the power of this "kindest Mother," Our Lady, "in the face of death."

The Air Force made three-day passes available once a month. I always took advantage of the offer and would eagerly drive the 420 miles home. The anticipation of seeing my mother, father, brothers and sisters spurred me on, making the drive an exhilarating breeze. The reverse was true when departure time came! Hugs, kisses, hand-shakes with heavy hearts and tears were unavoidable.

Generally I would stretch my time to the limit, leaving the last minute. The drive, in good weather, required 8 hours. Always I allotted 10 minutes for a visit to Our Lady of Guadalupe Church before attempting the return trip. A hurried dash into the Church, a blessing with holy water, a genuflection, a prayer to Our Lord in the Blessed Sacrament, and a little visit to His Mother on the side altar made up the visit. Before leaving, I would light a vigil candle to Our Lady—which I cherished doing—and pray three Hail Mary's imploring Her to guide me back safely.

One cold March evening I set out on my return earlier than normal due to the inclement weather. I prayed extra hard to Our Lady to get me back. The vigil light lit, the three Hail Mary's prayed—most devoutly and I was on my way. Wintry winds combined with freezing rain made the driving hazardous. All the way my Rosary was in my hand.

Near Logansport, Indiana, the roads froze over and became a glaring sheet of ice. Fatigued, I now found it most challenging just to keep my eye lids from closing. I must not fall asleep. Singing, opening the windows, playing the radio—nothing seemed to help. "I must not fall asleep" is the last thing I recall as the car went sliding, out of control, on the slippery ice, heading for a huge semi-truck standing on the side of the road with red flares all around. Before yielding to the sleep, I knew there simply was no way to escape crashing into that truck! At the last possible second, defying the inevitable, the car swerved by itself(?) and half-circled around the truck, straightening itself out as it went by. I was utterly amazed, almost breathless, as I awoke and realized what had taken place. "Thank you dear Lady, thank you dear Lady" was my repetitious prayer as I prayed it with a grateful heart.

In the summer of that same year, a Fr. Joseph Carol, Redemptorist, was to preach a nine-day mission at the Base. He was a powerfully built man with lungs and voice to go along. But he was as gentle as a mouse. I could appreciate why he was selected to preach missions on military bases—he was dynamic he was compelling.

Each evening the chapel was packed to capacity. Protestant ministers occupied the last two pews which had been reserved for them. Each evening the service consisted of a rosary, Benediction and a talk by Fr. Carol followed by confession for those who wished to go. For each service he gave a different talk: Life, Grace, Sin, Our Lady, death, Judgment, Heaven, Hell and Eternity. Grace flowed. Hearts melted. The confessional lines were lengthy.

In his talk on Our Lady and Her Rosary, he stressed "trusting Her." "Place yourself in Her Motherly hands and She will lead you to Christ and Heaven." With great conviction did he stress praying the Rosary daily. "Next to the Holy Sacrifice of the Mass, there is no prayer as powerful as the Rosary when you meditate upon its mysteries."

He quoted an impressive statement by St. Albert the Great,

> A Christian gains more merit by thinking or meditating on the passion of Our Lord Jesus Christ, then if he had fasted on bread and water every Friday for a whole year, or had beaten himself with his discipline once a week until the blood flowed, or had recited the whole Book of Psalms every day.

If this is so, then how great must be the merit that we gain by the Holy Rosary which commemorates the whole life and passion of Our Lord.

He also quoted Pope Pius IX,

Among all the devotions approved by the Church, none has favored by so many miracles as the devotion of the Most Holy Rosary.

And, lastly, he said Our Lady would greet us with a grace if we greet Her with the Hail Mary.

In one of his dreams, St. John Bosco saw his beloved former pupil of the Oratory, Dominic Savio. "My dear Savio, tell me, what comforted you the most at the moment of your death?" Dominic answered,

The one thing that consoled me most at the hour of my death was the assistance of the mighty and lovely Mother of the Saviour. Tell your sons never to forget to pray to Her as long as they live.

St. Maximilian Kolbe, canonized by Pope John Paul II on October 10, 1982 composed this beautiful prayer:

Let me praise you,
O Most Holy Virgin!
Let me praise you at my own cost.
Let me live, work, waste away and die
for You alone.
Let me contribute to your exaltation,
to your highest exaltation.
Permit that others may outdo my zeal
in glorifying you, O Mary, so that by
holy rivalry your glory may grow more
rapidly just as He wills it, Who raised
You above all creatures.
In You alone, God has been more adored
than in all the other saints.
For You, God created the world, and for You
He created me also
O let me praise You, most Holy Virgin Mary!

Every day, he offered the entire world to Mary for protection in Her arms. And before World War II, Maximilian wrote:

> Modern times are dominated by Satan and will be more so
> in the future. The conflict with hell cannot be engaged by
> men, even the most clever. The Immaculate alone has from
> God the promise of victory over Satan. She seeks souls that
> will consecrate themselves entirely to Her, that will become
> in Her hands forceful instruments for the defeat of Satan
> and the spread of God's kingdom.

To get back to the mission, I was so geared up from his talks after the first four days that I was determined not to miss any. I could hardly wait until the next one. However, I had to pull K.P. (Kitchen Police) one day. In order to make Fr. Carol's next service I had to juggle my hours around. It meant working at 3:00 a.m.—for 13 straight hours—'til 6:00 p.m. The service would begin at 7:30 p.m. which meant I would have but one hour to catch up on some much needed sleep, and freshen up before running over to the chapel.

Exhausted, I laid down in my bed. I prayed fervently three Hail Mary's for Our Lady to please wake me up at exactly 7:00 p.m. as I had no alarm clock in my room. I quickly fell into a deep slumber. At exactly 7:00 p.m. there was a rap, rap, rap on my door! I jumped out of bed, quickly opened the door, looked both ways down the long hall-way. No one!

One cold, wet, windy day in January, I overheard a number of my buddies, who worked in the office with me, discussing a big, upcoming event carried in the Air Force newspaper. Tommie Wiswell, the world's greatest checker player, was to put on a demonstration of his playing prowess for the benefit of the Air Force. Anyone who so desired could challenge him. He was to be accompanied by two other experts whom the U. S. Government had hired to entertain the servicemen.

I was above average in the game. I had played everyone at our squadron level and usually would win two out of three games. Sergeant Baker was the only player who could beat me consistently. And he did so with ease. However, I practiced until I could finally beat him. It was then that I quit playing the game. 18 months had elapsed since my victories over the Sergeant. I had not touched a checker in all that time.

As my friends read aloud, with great excitement, the article praising the great Tommie Wiswell, something happened inside of me that was peculiar. I felt most uneasy.

"I'd like to see this guy play—he is the greatest in the world" one buddy said. Another followed with "betcha he never loses a game—betcha nobody can beat him except God." "I can beat him!" And a death-like silence came over everyone. All were looking at one another in more or less disbelief. Then all eyes were on me. The statement was made with such conviction that my friends would say nothing. They beckoned with their eyes, facial expressions, and body language for me to continue on. Picking up their desire, I said, "Come over to the U.S.O. hall and watch me beat this world champion!" I could hardly believe I had spoken those words—but it was too late, the proclamation had been made. It was so unlike me. I was reticent by nature. I was more stunned having made the statement than they were having heard it.

When I entered the hall it was almost filled with eager people who were seeking autographs from this famous person. Large tables were set up in a square. Four checkerboards were placed on each of the tables with accompanying chairs for the challengers. Mr. Wiswell would walk around on the inside of the square and played sixteen simultaneous games. I heard someone remark, "He hasn't lost a game in a long, long time." Before he would play the games, he wanted to show just how gifted he was. I am sure it was a psychological way of frightening the challengers—and it worked!

He walked off into a distant corner some 75 feet away from the square of checkerboards. A blind-fold—a black cloth—was tied around his eyes as he stood, facing the corner, his back to the audience. One of the two experts would now play him a game. Unlike his challenger, Mr. Wiswell could not see the board. All 64 squares on the board were numbered. A third party—a volunteer from the audience—was asked to move Mr. Wiswell's checkers as he played the game. The volunteer would say to Mr. Wiswell, "Your opponent moves his checker on square 9 to square 14." Mr. Wiswell would promptly respond with a countering move saying, "move my checker on square 24 to square 19." And the entire game was played in this fashion with Mr. Wiswell besting his opponent. He received thunderous applause from the several hundred people witnessing.

What was even more shocking, after the game, he asked that all of the checkers be placed back on the board. He then, still standing in the corner blind-folded, called every move that was played in the game—and told his opponent where he made his bad moves! Another booming applause was his! All of my buddies were near me chuckling as they said, "And you are going to beat him!" I was amazed at how great this man really was. I knew I had not the slightest chance against him—especially since I had not played the game in a year and a half! However, I responded—and many heard me say—"yes, I am going to beat him!"

An excited lady, a bit obese, with a million-dollar smile, overheard my brash comment and was deeply amused. To her husband, tall and lanky, sporting a neat mustache, she said, "Let's keep an eye on this lad; he thinks he can beat Tommie." Her innocent comment was loud enough for Mr. Wiswell to hear.

It was now time to start the contests. Mr. Wiswell gave a little speech in which he said,

> Anyone who can beat me will be given an autographed book which I have just written on how to play checkers.

He went on to say,

> I will have to have the first move in every game.

I liked his first statement. His second sunk me. I thought I must have the first move to beat him or else I wouldn't stand a chance.

Tension was high as Mr. Wiswell stepped inside of the four, square tables. Mr. Wiswell was a short, stocky man of middle age. He had the deepest-set, most piercing, beady, eyes I had ever seen. Before every move he'd use those eyes to his great advantage by deliberately staring at his opponent. Then, with a slight smirk, he'd move a checker, always creating the impression that his move was infallible, invincible.

He looked at his first opponent, moved the first checker, moved to the next opponent and repeated the procedure until he had made the first lap. When he came to me, the first time, he stared at me for the longest while before moving that first checker. After his move, I felt the game was over—I didn't know how to counter it. All of my buddies were waiting for my move. Then something very strange happened. I felt inspired to call on the powerful Lady—the Blessed Virgin Mary—to play him. I knew She was more brilliant than any man who ever lived. I remember Fr. Maximilian Kolbe, O.F.M. saying, "Man's mind is finite, no matter how great their genius; their minds always fit into a hat. But the wisdom of Mary, or the Wisdom of God, is infinite."

She could beat Tommie Wiswell. Immediately, I closed my eyes placing both hands upon them, bent my head down, and commenced to pray a most devout Hail Mary—as though it were my last one prayed on this Earth—before every move. I was so convinced Our Lady would hear me—even for this checker game—that I knew, out of reverential respect for Her listening to me, it was necessary for me to black out all thoughts of the game, to forget Tommie Wiswell, to forget what my friends would think—and never to think I would lose. Each Hail Mary was prayed the slowest I had ever prayed in my entire life, all the while concentrating only on the one word that I was then saying. By the time I completed my first Hail Mary, Tommie was standing in front of me waiting for my first move. I did not feel a voice inwardly telling me to move any checker. I just moved the checker I naturally felt I should. He quickly moved his second and moved on to this next opponent. Again I repeated my little ritual, forgetting everything except the Lady I was asking to play the game for me. Mr. Wiswell was there waiting again. I made my second move. The game went along smoothly in this fashion. Soon opponents were out of the game as Mr. Wiswell beat them soundly.

I overheard one of the two experts, also playing, say, "Look at that kid (me) giving Tommie a battle." My heart began beating quicker as I knew he was having his problems with me.

Of the sixteen challengers, only one expert and myself were left! Mr. Wiswell, I could tell, was bewildered! Shortly I had him in a position where I took one of his checkers—he was dumbstruck. Never did I let up on the Hail Mary's—never did I speed them up! He had just eliminated the other expert—he now had 15 victories. I was the only one left, and I had a one-checker advantage over him.

Mr. Wiswell was flabbergasted when I took another checker from him—I now had a two-checker advantage. At this point, he had 3 checkers. I had 5. Mr. Wiswell saw me go into my little ritual not knowing what I was doing. He lost his composure and almost shouted out "You've got the game. What are you doing?' Little did he know I was praying to Our Lady to beat him. I was so excited when I finally took his last checker that I was on Cloud 9! My buddies were dumbfounded!

Mr. Wiswell wanted to autograph my book. He wrote the date in it and my name. He then wrote "May you win all your games in life."A young woman standing near said excitedly, "He is giving you an autographed book on how to play checkers after you just beat him. You should give him a book on how to play the game!"

Mr. Wiswell was most inquisitive. So were the other two experts as all three shot question after question at me.

I then challenged Mr. Wiswell to another game—just he and I and no one else. He suddenly became silent and expressionless. I sensed his reluctance. the crowd was enthralled. I went through my ritual invoking the Mother of God again—only this time I hurried through every Hail Mary and did not concentrate on each word. I was savoring the sweetness of that first victory more than concentrating in prayer for another win. The results? I tied him! Again, he was beside himself in wonderment.

As I have traveled the world over escorting the International Pilgrim Virgin Statue of Our Lady of Fatima, a number of people have asked me what is the greatest spiritual book I have? My answer: "Twentieth Century Checkers" by Tommie Wiswell. For that book—like no other—has taught me the importance, and the power, of the Hail Mary!"

Our Lady had a more important lesson in store for me. Immediately word had gotten back to the base about my success in the checker contests. Monday, after working hours, there were over a dozen people outside of my office, with checker-boards underneath their arms waiting to take me on! They came from all parts of the base.

Pride—the most horrible of sins—found a vacuum in me. At quitting time, 4:00 p.m., I started playing all challengers, after having escorted them to the recreation room. I informed everyone I would start by taking on the highest ranking officers first. Captain Wong was first, followed by

Lieutenants, Master Sergeants, right on down to P.F.C.'s. We played for 3 hours 'til 7:00 p.m. a total of 24 games had been played—I lost 23 of them! The one person I did manage to best was illiterate. I recall being upset and asking myself, after I did beat him, how did they ever let this guy into the service?

Our Lady taught me one of the greatest lessons of my life. With Her, I defeated the world's Champion—without Her, I could do nothing. I was undoubtedly the most embarrassed man in the service after dropping all of those games. I wanted to bask in a glory that was not mine—it was Our Lady's.

The checker experience taught me, like nothing else ever has, the power of the Hail Mary—and devotion to Our Lady. I now realized, therefore, how powerful the Holy Rosary is for it contains 53 Hail Mary's.

A book on Fatima was given to me by a friend who was quite religious. In the book Sister Lucia said:

> The Most Holy Virgin has given a new efficacy to the recitation of the Holy Rosary. She has given this efficacy to such an extent that there is no problem, no matter how difficult it is, whether temporal or above all, spiritual, in the personal life of each one of us, of our families, of the families of the world, or of the religious communities, or even of the life of peoples and nations, that cannot be solved by the Rosary. There is no problem, I tell you, no matter how difficult it is, that we cannot resolve by the prayer of the Holy Rosary.

I decided to put Sister Lucia's words to the test. I made a promise to Our Lady that if She would grant something, very special, that I wanted, I would pray the Rosary every day for the rest of my life. I started praying the Rosary daily for my intention when in no time, what I wanted—what I honestly felt would take Our Lady to obtain—was mine!

I then prayed the Rosary, faithfully, every day. At this

time, I was Staff Sergeant. I occupied a room with three
Protestants who were rowdies. I used to loop my Rosary
through itself around the bar of my bed nearest my head. At
night, I would kneel and pray my night prayers, very con-
scious of the fact that my three friends were observing me. It
took all of the courage I could muster to continue doing so
nightly. After the lights were out, I would slip my Rosary off
the bar and pray it in bed. I did this faithfully for over a year,
never missing a day.

One day I was assigned C.Q. (Charge of Quarters).
That entailed staying up all night from 8:00 p.m. until 8:00
a.m., and taking any emergency telephone calls that might
come from the Red Cross. You were given a pot of coffee—piping hot—and a batch of magazines to keep you
awake all through the night. When you completed the assigned 12 hours, you would receive the next 24 hours off.
During my night of duty, two emergency phone calls came
from the Red Cross. I was to awaken two servicemen to take
the messages on the phone. Proper arrangements having
been made, within hours they were on their way home.

In the evening of the next day I was preparing for bed. I
had been up over 30 straight hours without sleep. I enter-
tained the thought of sleeping the clock around. When I
went to my room, I was the only one there as my three ras-
cal-roommates were out painting the town red. Exhausted
and bleary-eyed, I knelt at my bed to say my night prayers
with my uniform still on. I fell asleep in the process. My
hands were on my eyes. My elbows on the bed. Several minutes elapsed before I awoke, startled. Only through sheer
will-power was I able to complete the night prayers. I then
glanced at my Rosary. I wondered how I could possibly pray
that Rosary in the condition I was in—my body was pleading
for slumber. Too tuckered out to remove my clothing, I slid
into my bed anticipating a well-deserved sleep. As I lay on
the bed, my conscience began to bother me. I heard a voice

say to me, "You promised Our Lady you would pray the Rosary every day if She granted your request!" Another voice followed up with, "But you are too tired and you need your rest!" The other voice came back with, "But a promise to the Mother of God is a promise to the Mother of God!" "You are only flesh and blood. You must be prudent. Get your rest!" Finally, before going off into a deep slumber I inwardly said to Our Lady—my conscience tormenting me all the while—"if that one Rosary makes that much difference to you, then give me a sign!" She did! Immediately my Rosary began to undo itself—very slowly—and fall to the floor! I jumped out of bed, picked my Rosary, and prayed the most devout Rosary I ever prayed in my life! I never batted an eye—I was no longer tired!

I returned to the book I had been given on the Lady of Fatima and read it again. I noted that Our Blessed Lady related World Peace to the simple praying of the Holy Rosary! Being in the service, and having access to the Base library, I began to do some research. Cardinal Spellman of New York was the Chaplain in command of all military branches in the U. S.

He had a great devotion to the Holy Rosary, and once stated that more Rosaries were prayed in the 6-year span, 1939 through 1945, than any other equivalent period previously. That being the case, I wondered what effect that many Rosaries had on the outcome of WWII. Here are some thought provoking facts I came up with after much research:

1. August 15, 1940, the greatest air battle ever fought in the history of the world took place over the skies of London when 27 squadrons of English Hawker-Hurricanes and Spitfires shot down 157 German aircraft badly crippling the Luftwaffe and putting an end to their "Operation Sea Lion" which was the secret code for the invasion of England. August 15 is the feast of the Assumption.

2. December 7th, 1941, Japan bombed Pearl Harbor in a

sneak attack. It was a day of infamy. The next day the U. S. officially declared war on Japan. December 8th is the feast of the Immaculate Conception. Our country is dedicated to Our Lady under Her title "The Immaculate Conception."

3. For two years, Germany, Japan and Italy were defeating Russia, England and the U. S. The turning point of the war came February 2, 1942, when the powerful German 6th Army under Field Marshall Von Paulist was crushed at Stalingrad by Marshall Zhukov. February 2nd is the feast day of the Purification of Our Lady.

4. May 13, 1943, the North African campaign came to a close when all German soldiers under Field Marshall Jurgen Von Arnim surrendered and all Italian soldiers under General Guiseppe Messe did likewise. May 13th is the feast day of Our Lady's first apparition at Fatima when She would ask the Rosary be prayed for World Peace.

5. September 8, 1943, Italy capitulated. September 8th is the Birthday of Our Lady.

6. May 13th, 1945, the U. S. government issued a proclamation in thanksgiving to God for victory over Germany. May 13, again, is Our Lady's first apparition at Fatima.

7. August 15th, 1945, Japan surrendered. World War II was over. August 15th is the feast day of the Assumption of Our Lady into Heaven.

8. September 2nd, 1945, the battleship Missouri with General Douglas MacArthur on board, received the unconditional surrender of the Japanese delegates. September 2, in that year, came on a first Saturday—Our Lady asked for the five first Saturdays to be made in reparation for sin.

9. September 8, 1945, the first American flag flew over Tokyo. September 8th, the Birthday of Our Lady.

Padre Pio is perhaps the most famous priest of this century. To our knowledge, he is the only person to whom Our Lord gave seven special gifts:

1. The gift of bi-location.
2 The gift of levitation.
3. The gift of heavenly fragrance.
4. The gift of the Stigmata.
5. The gift of discernment of spirits.
6. The gift of healing.
7. The gift of prophecy.

He said, in 1958, there were enough Rosaries being prayed to prevent a Third World War. He also said that when there was a person, in the world, doing what Our Lady of Fatima requested, for every communist, Russia would be converted and we would have an era of peace in the world.

An article written by an Italian priest for a Catholic magazine baffled me. I could hardly believe what I was reading. God's Holy Will saw that I would accompany the International Pilgrim Virgin Statue into the Hawaiian Islands in December of 1977. To my great joy, I would meet this priest who had written the article. I said to him, "I read your article and found it difficult to accept—was there a mistake in it?" "No, there was not!"

The story goes like this. Being a long-time acquaintance of Padre Pio's, and knowing that Padre Pio prayed a minimum of 15 five-decade Rosaries daily, the priest friend one day asked Padre Pio, "Padre Pio, did you pray 15 Rosaries today?" "I prayed more." "75, 100?" "More, more." "Did you pray 125 Rosaries?" "More." "Did you pray 135, 150?" "Some more." "160?" "Yes!" How could Padre Pio possibly pray 160 five-decade Rosaries in a 24-hour period? Mathematically it is impossible if you are going to do justice to the Rosaries. The priest replied, Padre Pio had the gift of bi-location and could be praying in two places at one time, if need be. He required little sleep, sometimes 2 hours per night.

As astonishing as Padre Pio's story is, I found another

that was equal to it. Bob Ripley, in his "Believe-it-or-not", tells the story of a Shah of Persia who had heard about the 15 promises to the Holy Rosary. He took a Rosary, wrapped it in his right hand, and that Rosary never came out of his hand for 43 years! Whether or not the Shah prayed the Rosary, Mr. Ripley does not say. But what a magnificent act of faith in Our Lady's Rosary. It reminds me of Christ and the Apostles. Matthew's 8th Chapter, 6th verse tells when Our Lord entered Capharnaum, a Roman Centurion—who was a pagan—approached Our Lord and said to him, "Lord, my servant is lying sick in the house paralyzed, and is grievously afflicted." Jesus said to him, "I will come and cure him." The centurion said, "Lord, I am not worthy that Thou shouldst come under my roof; but only say the word, and my servant will be healed." His words have become immortalized in the Holy Sacrifice of the Mass when we substitute the word soul for servant.

Jesus marvelled and said to those following him, "Amen, I say to you, I have not found such great faith in Israel." Likewise, I wonder, if Our Lady could look down upon earth from Heaven and say, "I have not found such great faith in my Rosary as this Shah of Persia."

During a visit to Springfield, Massachusetts, Mother Teresa of Calcutta urged the people to "Pray the Rosary every day; teach others to pray the Rosary."

The Rosary has been the hallmark of Catholic Devotion down through the centuries, and the Church has enriched it with many blessings and rich indulgences. Even non-Catholics have come to see and appreciate the beauty of the Rosary as a holy article and the prayer it represents, a fruitful meditation.

In the Cleveland area, many non-Catholics are praying the Rosary. One day, Bishop Cooper, the pastor of the Call Out Church of Almighty God in Elyria, Ohio went to the Daughters of St. Paul Book and Film Center to purchase needed supplies for his Church. In friendly conversation he lamented the evil and corruption in the world. He said: "I know you Catholics have something in your Church every day. I would like something each day in our church that we could do together."

"Why not say the Rosary?" Sister suggested. "This is a powerful prayer that will win blessings for your people and keep them away from evil."

Bishop Cooper decided to try, so he bought the booklets, "The Rosary Made Easy for Non-Catholics," the "Great Promise of Our Lady of Fatima," the "Secret of the Rosary", and a Rosary. Bishop Cooper asked his priest friend to explain the Rosary to his parishioners and to say it with them for the first time.

He soon kept returning to the Book Store for more and more Rosaries. He said, "Sister, I can't thank you enough for telling me about the Rosary. It's great! Since we started saying it we even got sixty-five new members. We have so many coming to our Rosary Service, that we had to schedule two services each day to accommodate them all!"

Mr. Cooper's wife too, grew to love the Mother of God. This is what she said: "I can't believe it! Here all these years we've been talking about Jesus and we've never said a word about His Mother. I asked my husband one Sunday if I could give the sermon and I told our people how important the Blessed Mother is in our lives. Why, She suffered in Her Heart every pain that Jesus suffered in His Body. She cooperated to save us!"

And Bishop Cooper added: "We would never give up the Rosary for anything. Ever since the Holy Queen came into our lives, I've noticed a change in the congregation. They're more outgoing than they were, more charitable toward each other."

The Call Out Church now has a statue of the Mother of God on the front lawn. It is Our Lady of Grace!

The Rosary

"So powerful, indeed, is the Blessed Virgin with God and his only begotten son that, as Dante observes, anyone who desires his help and fails to have recourse to Mary is like one trying to fly without wings."

(Pius XII to Cardinal Maglione, April 15, 1940)

What is the Rosary?

1. God's great holy picture book explained by his mother.
2. The little switch which closes the circuit between heaven and earth.
3. Heaven's bridle controlling the run-away earth.
4. The bell cord by which we call for heaven's help in danger or in need.
5. The mountain climber's supporting lifeline above the dizzy abyss.
6. The diadem of pearls with which Our Lady's coronation constantly recurs.
7. The bonds which bind us to the poor souls in purgatory and to sinners on earth.
8. The truly blessed child-harness and leash by which the mother of Him who wants us to be His children leads us to the eternal Father's home.
9. The portable transistor tuned to station MARY.
10. The television where on the screen of the Immaculate Heart, Christ is portrayed by the divine power of the Holy Spirit.
11. A tape-recording of the holy Gospels.
12. The typewriter where the paper with Mary as typist receives the impression of the keys which are Christ.

The word "Rosary' is taken from the Latin word rosarium which means a rose garden. Each time we pray the Rosary, we offer to the Mother of God, a cluster of roses, a garland of the most beautiful prayers, mingled with meditation on the most beautiful mysteries.

The Rosary is a powerful weapon to fight the evils of atheism and immorality. Yet it is the most sublime and simple of all prayers. It combines two methods of prayer—vocal and mental. It contains the most profound mysteries of Christianity.

Beginning with the Annunciation by the Archangel Gabriel to the Mother of God, it leads us in order through the sacred mysteries of the life, death and resurrection of Our Lord as related in the Gospel.

The vocal prayers—coming from God—are divine. The "Our Father" was composed by Our Lord Himself. How can the Father, when prayed to with the very words of His Son refuse to come to our aid? The "Hail Mary" begins with the eulogies of the Archangel Gabriel and St. Elizabeth, and ends with a pious supplication by which we beg the help of the Blessed Virgin now and at the hour of our death. The "Glory Be" is a profession and praise of the Blessed Trinity.

Cardinal Newman said,

> The great power of the Rosary consists in the fact that it translates the Creed into prayer. Of course, the Creed is already in a certain sense a prayer and a great act of homage towards God, but the Rosary brings us to meditate again on the great truth of His life and death, and brings this truth close to our hearts. Even Christians, although they know God, usually fear rather than love Him. The strength of the Rosary lies in the particular manner in which it considers these mysteries. Since all our thinking about Christ is intertwined with the thought of His Mother, in the relations between Mother and Son, the Holy Family is presented to us, the home in which God lived His infinite Love.

The Rosary is adaptable to every class of persons and to every order of intellect. It is a favorite prayer of clergy and religious. It is the daily practice of the Popes.

The beautiful "garland of roses" keeps before our mind the infinite love of the Father, who sent His only-begotten Son to redeem us, and the boundless love of the Son, who gave His life in paying our debt. It brings to mind the Holy Spirit, Whom He sent to dwell in our souls, and to guide His Church. And the reflection on these joyful, sorrowful and glorious mysteries keeps before us the pattern that God in His Providence intends for the life of each one of us, which too, will have its joys, sorrows and tribulations, all of which are meant to lead to glory. No prayer is more pleasing to the Father, or more powerful—if prayed with understanding and devotion—than the prayer which Jesus taught us; and you can offer Mary no prayer more pleasing than the greeting to Her which the Father placed on the lips of the Archangel Gabriel. These two prayers compose the body of the Rosary, a body brought to life with reflection on the sacred mysteries of our Redemption.

Carrying the beads is a sign of our august alliance with Mary. The succession of Hail Mary's that form the Rosary is a mysterious chain which unites us to Our Mother in Heaven; it is a spiritual ladder by which we may ascent to our celestial country. Astonishing miracles have manifested its power and efficacy. In his encyclical, *The Recitation of the Rosary to Combat Modern World Evils*, Pope Pius XI stated,

> The faithful of every age, both in public misfortune and in private need, turn in supplication to Mary, so that She may come to their aid and grant help and remedy against sorrows of body and soul. And never was Her most powerful aid hoped for in vain by those who besought it with pious and trustful prayer. . . . Among the various supplications with which we successfully appeal to the Virgin Mother of God, the Holy Rosary without doubt occupies a special and

distinct place. . . . If men in our century, with its derisive pride, refuse the Holy Rosary, there is an innumerable multitude of holy men and women of every age and every condition who have always held it dear. They have recited it with great devotion, and in every moment they have used it as a powerful weapon to put the demon to flight, to preserve the integrity of life, to acquire virtue more easily, and in a word to attain real peace among men.

How does Our Lady bless those faithful to Her Rosary? Fr. Gobbi, the founder of "The Marian Movement of Priests" said Our Lady told him through a locution that whoever prays a five decade Rosary daily, every member of their family will be saved! It seems that Fr. Solanus Casey, a Franciscan, who died in the odor of sanctity in Detroit in 1957, could confirm this thrilling statement. Fr. Casey used to have visions of throngs of souls climbing into Heaven. He wondered what was the ladder they were using. He looked closely and saw it was indeed, the Holy Rosary.

Almost at the same time that Senator Robert Kennedy, aspiring for the highest office of the land, was struck down mortally wounded by an assassin, and his last act of life—witnessed on national television—was to reach into his pocket, pull his Rosary out, and place it with his right hand, reverently, on his heart, as he took the last breath allotted him in this life, Fr. Gabriel Harty, O. P. was on national television in Ireland saying,

The person that takes a Rosary into his or her hand, commands more power than the President of the United States.

How badly does Our Lady want Rosaries? There is an old saying, "Actions speak louder than words." We can see how much She wants Rosaries by Her actions. Take three of Her recent apparitions to Earth, approved by Holy Mother Church, and watch Her actions. In the first one, Lourdes,

She appeared to a 14 year old peasant girl, St. Bernadette, with a Rosary over Her right elbow. She made 18 appearances from February 11 through July 16, 1858. She fingered the Rosary as Bernadette prayed it.

Go to the next apparition, Fatima, Portugal, 1917. The Rosary moves from Her right elbow to Her right hand, symbolic of, "take it and pray it." Just in case we miss the symbolism, She backed it up with "I want you to pray the Rosary every day!"

Apparently, we didn't get the message. Going to the next apparition, we find Our Lady appearing to five children: Fernande, Gilberte and Albert Voisin, 15, 13 and 11 years of age respectively, and to Andrée and Gilberte Degeimbre, 14 and 9 respectively, from the 29th of November, 1932 to the 3rd of January, 1933.

As many as 15,000 people would be present during some of the apparitions. When the children saw Our Lady, they would go into profound ecstasy and pray the Rosary most devoutly. Doctors present would stick pins into their flesh, and light cigarette lighters beneath their hands—they felt nothing nor was there any damage to their flesh.

After the apparitions, the children were questioned, 'Why did you pray the Rosary during the apparition?" "Because we had no alternative Our Lady forced us to pray the Rosary."

In the St. Paul Pioneer Press and Dispatch Newspaper of Friday, September 20, 1985, page 5-B, Walter Peyton, the National Football League's greatest all-time ground gainer, was asked the reason for the Chicago Bears catching afire and coming from behind to trounce the Minnesota Vikings. "I got my Rosary beads out at half-time." Frequently, when a desperation pass is thrown by a quarterback, announcers now refer to it as "The Hail Mary pass." And after a fabulous play is made by an athlete, and the cameras zoom in on the hero of the moment, he can be heard to almost say, "Hi

Mom", as he smiles at the T.V. audience.

The July-August, 1986 issue of *Queen* magazine carried a remarkable story of Bartolo Longo, born in Latiano, Italy, February 11, 1841 of good, Catholic parents. He lost his faith while attending the University of Naples in an era characterized by anticlericalism and opposition to the teachings and authority of the Pope. He fell victim to a satanic sect who ridiculed Bishops, priests and the rites of the Catholic Church. Feeling a strong desire to become a priest of Satan, he was permitted to be consecrated by a bishop of this sect. He wrote that during the ceremony the church of Satan became a true inferno. The walls shook with thunder, and there was lightning amid cries of blasphemy. Bartolo was so frightened that he fainted and remained in a state of insanity for some days afterward. His health was impaired greatly by this experience. For the rest of his life he suffered poor eyesight and digestive problems. Despite this experience he continued for some time to exercise the office of satanic priesthood by preaching, by officiating at rites, and by publicly ridiculing the Catholic Church.

God's grace touched Bartolo through a life-long friend of his home town, Vicente Pepe, who, in loving concern, brought back to Bartolo the memory of his parents' faith and their devotion to the Blessed Mother. Bartolo withdrew from the satanic sect, went to Confession and received Holy Communion.

One day, while in Pompeii, he felt the pangs of despair. Satan was desperately trying to convince him he was a priest of Satan for all eternity because of the consecration, and that there was a place in hell awaiting his arrival. His despair was so great that he contemplated suicide. Suddenly he heard this voice say, "If you seek salvation, promulgate the Rosary."

Needless to say, Bartolo did just that. The balance of his life he spent promoting Our Lady's Rosary. And the shrine to Our Lady of the Rosary at Pompeii has become the national shrine in Italy to the propagation of the Rosary in that country. Bartolo led a life of heroic sanctity as a layman. He died October 5, 1926. On October 26, 1980, in the Piazza of St. Peter's Basilica in Rome, with a gigantic painting of this former priest of Satan present, Pope John Paul II, proclaimed to the world by his infallible authority that this former worshipper and priest of Satan had, by transforming himself into an apostle of the Rosary, reached the beatific vision of heaven.

"A devotée of Mary will be saved; a great devotee of Mary will become a Saint!" said Rev. James Alberione, SSP, STD.

Archbishop Finbar Ryan of Ireland said Our Lady has 1600 titles! Isn't it electrifying that She would identify Herself to the children of Fatima by saying, "I am the Lady of the Rosary?" She could have called upon Her greatest, most exalted, title and said, "I am the Mother of God." She could have chosen Her second greatest title, "I am the Immaculate conception." On through 1600 titles! She chose "The Lady of the Rosary" to emphasize the importance and the necessity of the daily Rosary in our lives.

Pope Pius IX once conducted a tour through the Vatican. Many questions were posed to him. One was, "Your Holiness, of all the treasures in the Vatican, which is the greatest?" Some present in the pilgrimage thought surely he would single out the "Pieta" by Michelangelo—a priceless work of art. Others thought perhaps a painting by Leonardo da Vinci. The Holy Father reached into his pocked and removed a Rosary. Holding it high in the air, he answered, "This is the greatest treasure in the Vatican." He went on to say, at another time, "Give me an army praying the Rosary, and I will conquer the world."

Pope Saint Pius X, who gave us daily Holy Communion, said, "Give me one million families praying the Rosary and the world is saved." Pope Pius XI gave Rosaries away as wedding gifts. Pope Pius XII prayed the fifteen decade Rosary daily. Pope John Paul II wasted no time saying, "The Rosary is my favorite prayer." Pope John XXIII, who gave us Vatican II, in his five-year Pontificate from 1958 through 1963, spoke out 38 times on the Rosary. He prayed the fifteen decade Rosary daily. He wrote two encyclicals on the Holy Rosary, *Grateful Memories* and *The Holy Rosary*. He has fondly said, "O Blessed Rosary of Mary."

Fatima is essentially a Rosary apparition. The Blessed Virgin recommended the Holy Rosary in all six apparitions. When little Jacinta was asked, "What was Our Lady most insistent in recommending?"she answered, "The recitation of the Rosary every day." Thus Pope Pius XII in his radio address to the pilgrims at Fatima at the close of the silver jubilee of the apparitions, October 31, 1942, spoke especially of "The recitation of the Holy Rosary which was so earnestly recommended by Our Lady of Fatima."

Pope Paul VI wrote two encyclicals on the Rosary, *Rosaries to the Mother of God for World Peace* and *The Month of May*, urging us to pray the Rosary. In his exhortations, *Marialis Cultus*, he again talks about the importance of prayer to Our Lady. Pope Leo XIII was called the Rosary Pope because of the many encyclicals he wrote on the Rosary.

St. Clement Hofbauer would convert the hardest sinners by praying one devout Rosary for the soul. St. Francis de Sales was a most meek and most strong priest; a Bishop of inexhaustible zeal; a writer and preacher of true devotion; a marvel because of his prodigies. Why? He overcame the hardest trials by making a vow to recite the entire Rosary daily, and he kept his vow faithfully. He wanted to retire with his two greatest weapons, at the age of 54, the Rosary and his pen!

Years ago there was a popular song that caught on all

over the country, "Red Roses for a Blue Lady." this Blue Lady, the Mother of God, doesn't want roses—She wants Rosaries, Rosaries and more Rosaries! Perhaps that is why Bishop Sheen would remark, "Do you want to know what the trouble in our chaotic world is? There are not enough Rosaries being prayed!"

When the Bishop was about to decide on the ordination of the future Cure of Ars, he hesitated because Saint John Marie Vianney had very little ability in his studies. But then the Bishop asked, "Do you know how to say the Rosary?" "Oh yes, very well," he replied. And then the Bishop said, "We will ordain him. He will be a good priest." And seldom has a priestly life been so holy, self-sacrificing, so fruitful of good for the salvation of souls as the life of St. John Marie Vianney, the Cure of Ars, who is the patron saint of parish priests. He spent 16 to 18 hours a day in the confessional setting consciences aright and softening hardened souls. He conducted a catechetical instruction in Church every day, and insisted upon the recitation of the Rosary which he personally led.

One of the most awe-inspiring sights I have ever witnessed was escorting the International Pilgrim Virgin Statue to the Philippines, where, at Luneta Park, in Manila, two million people prayed the Rosary to resolve the problems of their land. It was an astonishing, bloodless, victory as Marcos had been ousted through prayer—the Rosary!

St. John Baptist de LaSalle was called the man of the Rosary—it was never out of his hands. The same was true of St. Francis Regis!

Called the "Magnifier of Mary," there can be little doubt that one of the greatest apostles of Mary of this century was Frank Duff, the founder of the Legion of Mary. He focused world attention on the greatness of the Blessed Virgin Mary and Her role in the economy of salvation.

His work and the work of the Legion he founded have

been praised by five Popes and the innumerable Cardinals,
Bishops and priests all around the world. At the Second
Vatican Council, which he was invited to attend as a lay ob-
server, when he was introduced by Cardinal Heenan, the
2,500 prelates rose to their feet and greeted him with a pro-
longed applause. Three days later, Pope Paul VI spoke with
him in a private audience saying,

> Mr. Duff, I want to thank you for your services to the
> Church, and also to express appreciation for all that the Le-
> gion of Mary has done . . . The Legion of Mary has served
> the Church faithfully . . .

Frank Duff always maintained that the Rosary was of
paramount importance to his life and work.

Since the age of 5, St. Louis de Montfort, called "The
extraordinary preacher of the Rosary," recited it daily with
fervor. He found it a most powerful instrument in his struggle with Satan for the souls of men. He would tell his fellow
priests,

> I could tell you at great length of the grace God gave me to
> know by experience the effectiveness of the preaching of the
> Holy Rosary, and how I have seen with my own eyes the
> most wonderful conversions it has brought about. I assure
> you that the Rosary is a priceless treasure which is inspired
> by God.

And to everybody who listened he told them,

> I earnestly beg of you to say the Rosary every day. When
> death draws near, you will bless the day and hour when you
> took to heart what I told you, for, having sown the blessings
> of Jesus and Mary, you will reap eternal blessings in heaven.

St. Louis IX, King of France, recited the Rosary even
while leading his army in times of war. St. John Berchmans

died clutching the crucifix, the Rosary, and the Rules of his Order. "These were the three things dearest to me during my life," he kept saying, "with these I die happily."

It has been stated, "With the Rosary, Daniel O'Connell saved Ireland from England's oppression."

St. Alphonsus de Liguori would interrupt any activity at the sound of the church bells to say the Hail Mary. St. Catherine of Siena began at the age of 5 to recite as many Hail Mary's as the number of steps she climbed. St. Bernard said that Mary is the Mediatrix of all graces. He said, "Mary is the neck through which every grace descends from the head to the members of the body."

Blessed Beneventua Bojani used to say, as a child, 1,000 Hail Mary's each day to Our Lady; 2,000 on Saturdays plus saying 700 Our Fathers and 700 Hail Mary's, making a different intention for each 100 prayed.

Blessed Margaret of Hungary, O.P. had the custom of reciting prostrate on the ground 1,000 Our Fathers on vigils of feast days of Our Lord, and 1,000 Hail Mary's on the eve of feasts of Our Lady.

Quoting St. Louis de Montfort again,

> When the Hail Mary is said with attention, devotion and modesty, it is a hammer against the devil, the sanctification of souls, the joy of angels, the melody of the predestined, the canticle of the New Testament, the delight of Mary and the glory of the Blessed Trinity.
> The Hail Mary is a heavenly dew which renders the soul fertile; it is a chaste and loving kiss bestowed on Mary; it is a deep red rose presented to Her; it is a precious pearl offered to Her; it is a chalice of divine nectar lifted to Her lips.

The early 1800's, a University student riding a train going from Dijon to Paris, France found himself seated next to a person dressed in peasant clothing, praying his Rosary and slowly moving the beads through his fingers.

The student interrupted the old man asking, "Sir, do you still believe in such outdated things? Take my advice and throw the rosary out the window, and learn what science has to say about it." "Science? I do not understand this science. Perhaps you can explain it to me", the man humbly requested.

The student saw that the man was deeply moved and replied, "Give me your address and I will send you literature to help you on this matter." The man fumbled in the inside of his coat pocket and gave the young student his card. On glancing at the card, the student bowed his head in shame and became silent. The card read: "Louis Pasteur, Director of the Institute of Scientific Research, Paris, France."

Louis Pasteur was one of the greatest scientists of the 19th century, and the founder of modern bacteriology. His name has become immortalized through the process we know as pasteurization.

I used to visit an elderly lady in a convalescent home on a regular basis. She was as beautiful on the inside as she was on the outside. Nellie Chisholm, now in her golden years, always had her Rosary near. It was her most precious treasure. Shortly before God called her into eternity, she gave me that Rosary. She had purchased the rosary in St. Louis, Missouri, in the 1920's, and had prayed it faithfully ever since. Praying on the beautiful purple-beaded Rosary, one can almost feel Nellie's fingers joining your own as you move from bead to bead.

Many years ago I was working in a small manufacturing shop operating a metal lathe. Something powerful came over me and I was almost forced to follow the instructions. It was made known to me that I should turn off the power of the machine, clean up, and make a visit to a holy lady who lived in our town, Mary Brown. Within 10 minutes I was hastily parking my car in her drive by a patch of wild flowers. I noticed her sitting in a lawn chair, covered with blankets, absorbing the warm sun. The rays of the sun were therapeutic for her frail, ailing body. Sheepishly I said, "Mary, I don't know why I am here." With an angelic smile, and quiet and most pleasing manner, her Rosary in her right hand, she cheerfully said, "I prayed my Rosary that Our Lady would send you to me at this time. I wanted to see you." she said, as she measured each word because of one lung. Our Lady had arranged one of the most beautiful, peaceful visits I would ever know.

At the Monastery of Our Lady of the Rosary in Buffalo, New York, the Dominican Nuns of the Perpetual Rosary pray the Rosary 24 hours a day in the chapel. The nuns take turns rising throughout the night to pray the Rosary for an hour.

Mother Angelica wrote a nifty little booklet, *My Life in the Rosary*. On the inside of the cover she states, "The author prays these meditations will make the Rosary a friend in need."

While escorting the International Pilgrim Virgin Statue of Our Lady of Fatima throughout the state of South Carolina, I took the image to the Oratorian Fathers in Rock Hill. The good priests were kind enough to show me the precious Rosary that once belonged to St. Philip Neri. Seeing how moved I was by the privilege of holding the Rosary in my hands, the prior said, "If you like, you can take the Rosary into the chapel and pray on it!" "God bless you for your wonderful kindness"—and I was running to the chapel with a treasure that would be mine for the next thirty minutes. Holding each bead was an unbelievable joy as I prayed as devoutly as I possibly could. This was one Rosary that I did not want to see end. The Rosary completed, I returned the treasure to its source.

Shortly after this experience, a situation came into my life, unexpectedly, that required a major decision. After praying for one week, I was boarding a plane from Flint,

Michigan to Los Angeles with Our Lady's image. The flight would take 5-1/2 hours. I still hadn't received an answer to my prayers. I decided to spend that entire flight praying one "Hail Mary" after the other without let-up. I begged Our Lady, half way through the flight, to have someone present me with a red rose upon my arrival at the L.A. airport if the choice were to be where my heart was leading me, and to have someone present me with a white rose if it was to be what Our Lady wanted.

Our D-10 touched down gently on the runway. In a few minutes, with the statue in my arms, I was walking into the terminal to be welcomed by a huge throng of people. A black haired, Oriental woman, was the first one to greet me by stepping forward and pinning a white rose on the lapel of my dark blue suit. It was the first time that anyone ever pinned a white rose to my suit. The issue was settled. Our Lady had given me Her answer.

Several times during the month's visitation in the L. A. diocese I saw this woman in different churches. I made it a point to ask her, after introducing myself, "Why did you pin a white rose on my lapel?" "Because Our Lady enlightened me to do so." "Why white, why not red?" "This is the color Our Lady wanted you to have!"

Father Gino Burresi lives near Rome at San Vittorino where Our Lady of Fatima appeared to him. She asked him to build a shrine there in Her honor. Like Padre Pio before him, he bears in his body, the five Wounds of Christ. He said,

> Our Lady has insistently stressed the recitation of the Holy Rosary as a prayer. The world's situation today is so sad! Love is hard to find, and charity, goodness, and justice are sluggish; the dignity of the human person is fading fast. Today, people talk only of rights, money, well-being; and they ignore the spiritual values . . . In the Rosary we have the Bible, the Prophets, the life of Jesus and Mary, the life of a Christian, and that of a Religious. Therefore, I would call

the Rosary "the scourge of Satan." We need to say the Rosary many times and we need to say it well. Don't pay any attention to those people, even if they are priests, who tell you otherwise.

Little Francisco, in his illness, prayed seven Rosaries a day! This small boy was able to remain in the presence of the Lord with the Rosary.

Not infrequently, and always with spine-tingling chills, do I recall an experience that happened over twenty years ago. Our former pastor, Fr. William M. Gannon, was spending his last days in St. Joseph's Hospital, as the sands of time were rapidly running out on his life. In his eighties, very sharp, very direct, his eyes looked like blue flames. Being a member of the St. Vincent de Paul Society, we were asked to visit him whenever possible.

After my first visit, I promised I'd try to spend some time with him every night. Due to working overtime, I was not able to see him during visiting hours. I used to sneak into the hospital through a basement door, generally arriving at 10:00 p.m. He was always happy to have a visit. Sometimes he would berate me for not coming sooner. Always he had his Rosary on his night stand or in his fingers.

One night I entered his darkened room and saw him sobbing copious tears. I tried to console him by telling him what a tremendous reward would be his for the beautiful years of service he had given God through the priesthood. I went into detail describing the judgment scene and how well it would go for him. He stared ahead, unblinking, as if pondering what I was saying. More tears flowed freely as he shook his head negatively. He winced as if experiencing pains of regret. I gave him a relic of Matt Talbot and promised to pray many Rosaries for him.

During one of the visits, I reluctantly told him that it would be several days before I would see him again as my

Father wanted me to go to his cottage in Tawas, Michigan for the weekend to help with some necessary work. I left Fr. Gannon, his Rosary in his hands, on a Thursday night close to midnight, praying "Hail Mary" after "Hail Mary" for him as I drove away.

Friday evening I was driving 120 miles north to the cottage praying one Rosary after another for Fr. Gannon. Often I was distracted by visions of myself basking in the warm sun, frolicking in the cool water, and taking in large gulps of the pure, fresh air that would come off of Lake Huron as I would view the lovely scenery from a power boat.

After we worked most of the day, Dad and I were in the cottage chatting from 8:00 p.m. 'til midnight about his boyhood life. His stories were so fascinating. When I retired it was 1:30 a.m. and I found it difficult to fall asleep as I recounted all of the interesting incidents in my Father's life. I fell asleep around 3:00 a.m. Before doing so, I had set the alarm clock for 7:50 a. m. The local church was not that far and I could awaken quickly, dress, throw some water into my face, comb my hair, and make it on time for the 8:00 a. m. Mass.

Into a very deep and strange sleep I went. I was stunned by a most vivid panorama manifesting itself to me that was real, not a dream! I was standing on one side of an enormous abyss that no one living could possibly cross over. I was a spectator. Into my view, from the other side of the abyss, I saw Our Lady walking Fr. Gannon to the judgment seat of Almighty God. I trembled. I saw the Trinity with flaming Seraphim all around. And there stood Fr. Gannon, Our Lady at his side, holding a large crutch underneath his right arm. I was breathless as I observed. His sentence was pronounced in a flash! Our Lady was now leading Fr. Gannon to Purgatory. After he entered, I shook with fear. It was awesome. Then I saw a sea of humanity too numerous to be numbered. It appears as though they were all of the souls in eternity. They too, had witnessed the sentence, or else, they would be the sight one would see at the General Judgment. I wanted to get away from this scene as quickly as possible to make hurried atonement for my own sins—I was frightened like I have never been.

My alarm clock went off: 7:50 a.m. The first thing I was struck with, powerfully, was that everything was not a dream. It did happen. And it all took place in a split second at precisely 7:50 a.m. I dressed, washed, combed my hair in a dither. My heart pounded fast. I was still in fright. All during the Mass I could not concentrate on anything except the experience of 7:50 a.m. I prayed many Rosaries that day.

On Monday I was back in Mt. Morris to attend our weekly St. Vincent de Paul meeting held in the evenings. One of our members, Mr. Robert Fournier, who worked at St. Joseph's Hospital, asked me for a ride home after the meeting. On the way, I said to him, "I've got to go and see Fr. Gannon tonight, I haven't seen him for a number of days." Somewhat astonished Robert said, "Haven't you heard? Fr. Gannon died last Saturday morning!" He continued, "I was just outside of his room when he passed away." "What time did he die?" I mumbled in a voice barely audible. "Exactly at 7:50 a.m." A cold chill encompassed my entire body.

St. John Bosco was very much aware of Mary's role in the plan of God in the cosmic struggle against evil. Emphatically he stated,

> I stand very much by the Rosary, and I may add that my Institute is founded on it. I would never abandon the recitation of the Holy Rosary.

The late Cardinal Faulhaber, Archbishop of Munich, said of his love for the Rosary,

With so much reading of newspapers, with so much listening to the radio, with the continual unrest that surrounds us, with the hectic pace of modern life, we are in great danger of becoming shallow and superficial. A silent Our Father may serve to bring us a moment's deep reflection. I confess that when my head is tired with the manifold duties of my daily work, and at last in the evening when I say the Rosary with my household, repeating fifty times the same Hail Mary and meditating on those mysteries of our Redemption that are ever old and ever new, I find a true rest for my mind. It is as if the Mother of God lays Her hand on the tired head and strokes the weariness away. Prayer is an art of living which the unbeliever cannot know.

Mr. Stephen Oraze, founder and editor of *Divine Love* magazine, was an outstanding apostle of Christian action. He placed great emphasis on traditional, Catholic devotion, especially the Holy Eucharist and the Rosary. He was in the forefront promoting the Rosaries for Peace Crusade.

On October 22, 1986, in the Annual "Rosaries for Peace" rally, Bishop Joseph Lawson Howze and the people of the Biloxi Diocese of Mississippi, dedicated the rally to Sister Ignatius McCarthy, R.S.M. with these heartfelt words on their program,

> We dedicate this rally to Sister Ignatius with love, respect and gratitude. Sister Ignatius, through her example, has reawakened the Mississippi Gulf Coast to the beauty and spiritual richness of the Holy Rosary and the message of Fatima.

Perhaps the greatest book on the Rosary is St. Louis de Montfort's "Secret of the Rosary" which has gone through 23 printings in 19 years and sold over two million copies in the U. S. alone.

Pope Urban IV testified, "The Rosary daily obtained fresh favors for Christendom." Don Juan ascribed the triumph of his fleet at Lepanto to the powerful intercession of the Queen of the Most Holy Rosary, and the Venetian Senate wrote to the other states which had taken part in the Crusade:

> It was not generals nor battalions nor arms that brought us victory; but it was Our Lady of the Rosary.

Pope Sixtus IV declared that the Rosary "redounded to the honor of God and of the Blessed Virgin, and was well fitted to impending dangers." Pope Leo X said, the Rosary was instituted to crush heresiarchs and growing heresies. Pope Julius III called it "the glory of the Church." Pope Saint Pius V declared "With the spread of the Rosary, the faithful have become more fervent by these meditations and more inflamed by these prayers, and that they have become different men, that the darkness of heresy has been dissipated, and the light of Catholic Faith has again beamed forth." Pope Gregory XIII said, "The Rosary was instituted by St. Dominic to appease the anger of God and to implore the intercession of the Blessed Virgin Mary." Pope Gregory XVI called the Rosary "A wonderful instrument for the destruction of sin, the recovery of God's grace, and the advancement of His glory."

St. Charles Borromeo attributed the conversion and sanctification of the faithful of his diocese to the devotion of the Rosary. He, as the Bishop of his diocese, ordered all priests to have a statue of Mary in a prominent place outside of the Church where all could see her.

St. Sharbel Makhloof of Lebanon was canonized by pope Paul VI, October 9, 1973. He died Christmas Eve, 1898—to this day his body is incorrupt. He used to spend two hours in thanksgiving after Mass. His great devotion was the Eucharist and the Rosary. Pope Paul VI called him "The Man of the Rosary."

The worst heresy the Church ever knew was the Albigensian. It discarded the doctrines of Christianity and offered new doctrines that played havoc with morality and social order. The Albigensians preached disobedience and rebellion against spiritual and temporal authority. The history of the Church has always shown that an enemy of the Church is invariably an enemy of the state.

St. Bernard spoke of the ramifications of this heretical sect,

> The Churches are empty, the people without priests, the Sacraments without reverence. People on their deathbed refuse the assistance of the Church and ridicule penance.

St. Dominic would be the tool in the hand of God to bring about an efficacious remedy to this heresy which was expanding throughout southern France by leaps and bounds. Pope Innocent III asked St. Dominic to go and preach against the errors of this heresy. Dominic preached but to no avail—their hearts were hardened. While in Toulouse, in 1214, Dominic prayed to Our Lady for a solution. She appeared to him and gave him the Rosary, and bade him preach it as an antidote to heresy and sin. He preached this devotion teaching the people how to pray it. In all the cities where he preached, the people gathered in huge numbers to be touched by his heaven-inspired words and pray the Rosary with him. Sinners converted. Many thousands who had left the Church returned. Historians of the day say that over 100,000 souls were brought back to the true faith, and the conversion of many notorious sinners testified to the power of the Rosary with the result that this new form of prayer was adopted by all of Christendom.

How applicable are the words of St. Alphonsus de Liguori,

> The walls of Jericho did not collapse more quickly at the trumpet call of Joshua than false teachings disappear after

the earnest praying of the Rosary. The swimming pool of Jerusalem was not as healing for the bodily sick as the Rosary is a remedy for the spiritually diseased.

Blessed Alan says that a nun who had always had a great devotion to the Holy Rosary appeared after death to one of her sisters in religion and said to her "If I were allowed to go back into my body, to have the chance of saying just one single Hail Mary—even if I said it quickly and without great fervor—I would gladly go through the suffering that I had during my last illness all over again, in order to gain the merit of this prayer."

When we read St. Louis de Montfort's words,

My Hail Mary, my Rosary of the fifteen or of five decades, is the prayer and the infallible touchstone by which I can tell those who are led by the Spirit of God from those who are deceived by the devil. I have known souls who seemed to soar like eagles to the heights, by their sublime contemplation, and who yet were pitifully led astray by the devil. I only found out how wrong they were when I learned they scorned the Hail Mary and the Rosary which they considered as being far beneath them.

Are we not reminded of St. Paul's words to St. Timothy:

For there shall be a time when they will not endure sound doctrine; but, according to their own desires, they will heap to themselves teachers, having itching ears; and will indeed turn away their hearing from the truth, but will turn to fables. (2 Tim. 4: 3-4)

People in all walks of life have found the Rosary to be a sustaining influence, especially through crisis situations. In 1970 Maryknoll Bishop James Edward Walsh was released from a 20 year sentence in a Chinese prison. He had been interned when the Communists took over. His return was national news and a joyous occasion. Besides saying that the only thing that kept his sanity was the reciting of the Rosary, he said,

> My constant ever-present companion was the Rosary. It ministered to my deepest need by making it feasible and easy for me to occupy myself with one of life's most important and rewarding activities—paying attention to God and communication with Him in prayer.

On various occasions St. Anthony Claret had been blessed by direct messages—in word—from the Blessed Mother. "You must be the Dominic of these times in propagating devotion to the rosary." In a sermon on Our Lady he said,

> If the enthusiasm with which I speak of the glories of my Most Holy Mother Mary surprises you, know, it could hardly be less, inasmuch as all my life long, She has been my Protectress, and even at this instant She is freeing me from a greater danger that threatens me.

Soon after delivering this sermon a man knelt before him, remorsefully extending the dagger with which he intended to kill St. Anthony.

Rev. Rawley Myers, Ph.D., former editor of the *Southern Nebraska Register* said in the May, 1987 issue of *Homiletic and Pastoral* review,

> Smart alecks in religion tell us the Rosary is old-fashioned and a peasant prayer. Well, the people, the ordinary Catholics, wiser than many of the "experts", love it, and so do I. And the Rosary is a good thing to fall back on. At least in saying this prayer, a person is praying and not just sitting and waiting for inspiration that never comes. In fact, in meditating on the mysteries of the Rosary, we think a good deal of Jesus.

Mary has been the object of ill-concealed persecution. Bruno Cornacchiola was a Protestant who hated the Blessed

Virgin Mary. On April 12, 1947, Our Lady appeared to this tramway conductor at Tre Fontane, Italy. She was moved with compassion towards this erring son of Hers. He was enraptured by Her indescribable beauty! Her countenance reflected maternal kindness, though penetrated by a serene look of sadness. He was forced to his knees, and with ecstatic rapture, clasped his hands in prayer. With incomparable Motherly kindness, She said to him:

> You persecute me. Now, that is enough. Now you must enter within the Sacred Fold of my Heavenly Court on Earth immediately.

Bruno knew he was to become a Catholic. She continued:

> Pray, pray very much. Pray a great deal. Recite the Holy Rosary every day for the conversion of sinners; for the incredulous; and for the unity of Christians.

How great was Bruno's hatred of Mary and the Catholic Church can be evidenced from the fact that he had engraved upon his dagger, "Death to the Pope."

In Bruno, Our Lady saw all of her children represented, whom She is trying to save in this critical hour of the human race.

Fr. Patrick Peyton, CSC, the Rosary priest, has said,

> I fight for the Rosary not as a fanatic or a lunatic, but with the knowledge that if I have Mary's hand knocking with mine, if I have Her eyes searching with mine, then the door will open and we will find what I need. God cannot take that lightly. And She would not be human if She did not help us when we ask.

Is the "Hail Mary" meant for all Christians? Rev. Donald Charles Lacy, pastor of Salem United Methodist Church in Hebron, Indiana, answers with a resounding yes! He continues,

> It is majestically simple and filled with ongoing insight. Is it
> Biblical? Yes. It meets the spiritual needs of praise and
> petition. It shows God's pleasure with Mary and His work in
> Her. Yet, with all of this praise of Her, we—in re-
> flection—discover She points to Her Son and in reality find
> homage paid to Her is dependent on Him. Will we someday
> find the "Hail Mary" in hymnals and books through the
> Faith? I fully expect this to happen, continues Dr. Lacy, be-
> cause the Blessed Mother is the key to authentic ecumenism
> in our day and time.

St. Clement Hofbauer assures us,

> When I am called to a sick man of whom I know that he is
> averse to making his peace with God, on the way I pray my
> Rosary, and when I reach him, I am sure to find him very
> desirous to receive the Sacraments.

Saint Benedict Joseph Labré embraced a life of volun-
tary poverty. He ate nothing but the fragments which he received as a poor beggar and esteemed himself happy in suffering hunger, thirst, and all the inconveniences of traveling;
for he had ever before his eyes the mortified life of the Most
Holy Virgin. He wore Her Rosary around his neck, praying
the fifteen decades daily. People were moved observing him
praying so devoutly before an image of Our Lady. He loved
to frequent Her shrines, of which the Holy House of Loretto
was his favorite.

He was often found at a very early hour at the gate of
the Church of Our Lady of the Mountains at Rome, in
which, during the eight years of his residence in that city, he
daily spent many hours motionless on his knees, more like an
angel than a man. In the beginning of 1783, he consecrated
to the Mother of God all the moments of that year, which
was to be his last. On the Wednesday in Holy Week, he went
to pray at the gate of his favorite Church of Our Lady of the

Mountains. He suddenly felt an excessive languor come over him, and fainted on the steps of the Church. He was brought into a house in the neighborhood, where some zealous religious followed him to administer the last consolations of religion. They began to pray, and at these words, "Holy Mary, pray for him," the faithful servant of Mary calmly rendered his soul to God without any difficulty.

There can be no better illustration of the protecting powers of Mary than that afforded to St. Ignatius of Loyola, the founder of the Society of Jesus. He offered himself first to Mary, and most earnestly pleaded Her to present and recommend him to Her Divine Son. As he was one night kneeling before Her image, and with tears, imploring Her to be his Protectress, the Holy Virgin with Her Divine Son appeared to him and this vision produced the most extraordinary change in his interior life. He constantly carried about him a picture of the Mother of God and in all difficulties and undertakings had recourse to Her intercession. He was careful to inspire all his disciples with a tender devotion to this Virgin Mother, that they might be assisted by Her protection in all their undertakings. One day, Father Araoz, his relative, on taking leave of him, manifested great regret at the separation. Ignatius, to console him, presented him with an image of the Holy Virgin, which he had carried around his neck, and assured him, that in all dangers of soul and body, he had constantly experienced the protection of Mary.

Called "The Friend of the Poor Souls," St. John Macias, O.P., of Lima, Peru, prayed three Rosaries every night for the suffering souls in Purgatory, kneeling all the while. St. John the Evangelist, whom he loved dearly, revealed to him that he had released more than one million souls from Purgatory through His Rosary. St. John knew it was a holy and wholesome thought to pray for the dead as did the faithful Macabees in Biblical times.

Called the "Apostle of Rome", St. Philip Neri's

devotion to the Mother of God was remarkable. He loved Our Lady so dearly that He had Her name almost always in his mouth, and incessantly labored to promote Her honor among men. No child ever had so tender an affection for his Mother as Philip had for Mary, whom he called "his love," "joy," and "consolation." He spoke these words with so much feeling and unction that those who heard him were usually deeply affected, and frequently moved to tears. He spent whole nights in prayer; and in his addresses to the Holy Virgin, he spoke with as much confidence and fervor as if She were actually present. He often was favored with supernatural visions of this celestial Queen. He walked the streets of Rome with his Rosary in his hand.

Often he told people,

> Believe me, there is no more powerful means to obtain God's grace, than to employ the intercessions of the Holy Virgin. Say to Her often: 'Virgin Mary, Mother of God, pray to Thy dear Jesus for me.'

An experience I had while in basic training at Lackland Air Force Base, San Antonio, Texas, convinced me that Our Lady indeed is the most powerful means to obtain God's grace. One week before Easter, April of 1951, all Catholics were urged to go to Confession. Enlisting together from Flint, Michigan, Jack Serbic and I naturally chummed around together. Into our fourth week of basic training, and having completed our "G.I. party" (scrubbing the floors of the barracks on our hands and knees with brushes and soap) I asked him to go to confession with me. Looking stressed he curtly replied, "I haven't been to confession in five or six years." "That is all the more reason why you should go." "I am afraid to go." "Come on." "No!" He was piqued and stiffened with fear.

Walking away, I took my Rosary from my pocket and prayed it for him. Fifteen minutes later I was back challenging him, "You better go Jack." I kept insisting. The more I persisted, the more he resisted. Finally, I blurted out a bit adamantly, "Okay, Jack, have it your way—but you could be dead in six months!" With that statement a dramatic change came upon him. In fifteen minutes we were in the back of the chapel. With anxious voice I said to him "Wait here and I will talk to the chaplain and soften him up for you." I begged the priest to be compassionate. He smiled, nodding his head approvingly. In minutes a trembling Jack walked into the confessional, only to come out radiant with joy. One could not deny the great serenity in his heart which reflected in his face. Confession was the balm his frazzled spirit needed. Now the sun was warmer, colors brighter, air fresher, for his life was in order, teeming with happiness.

Soon our training was completed. Jack was sent to Lorry Air Force Base, Denver, Colorado to receive advanced training in gunnery, while I was to go to State College, Pennsylvania, for training in office work. We corresponded weekly. A furlough was planned for December 10th. We could hardly wait to be reunited. In all of Jack's letters he would talk about his return to the Sacraments, his love of the Rosary, and his new found peace of mind.

One unusually warm December 3rd, 1951, I picked up my mail from home and dashed to the P.X. where I would enjoy a cup of coffee while reading my mail. I was thinking, 7 more days and I would be with my family and Jack. One rather heavy letter with additional postage from my Mother aroused my curiosity. Quickly I tore it open while the song "Shrimp Boats are Coming" was being played in the P.X. Unfolding the first page of the second section of our hometown newspaper, the *Flint Journal*, I froze with horror as I saw a large picture of Jack Serbic with the caption above, "Flint Airman killed in Denver crash." He was dead 8 months after I was inspired to tell him, "You could be dead in 6 months."

Distraught over the loss of my best friend, I was on my way to my new assignment: Chanute Air Force Base, Rantoul, Illinois. All processing completed, I was assigned to a new barracks with four men occupying the rooms. In the room next to mine, acts of immorality took place. I used to fall asleep praying the Rosary for the perpetrator of these evil deeds. He was a Catholic and had been away from the Sacraments for years. His actions were overlooked by those in authority due to the fact that he was a genius with outstanding organizational ability and skill—he was indispensable.

This man continued in his sinful ways for years. One brilliant, sunny Sunday, four days before I was to be discharged, I barged into his room and shook him from his sleep saying, "You are going to Mass this morning whether you like it or not!" It was 10:00 a.m. Startled, he jumped out of bed. I stared him in the face with determination. He responded with fear and alarm. There was an unholy dread in his voice as he broke the silence with, "I'd be the laughing stock of the base if I'm seen in church." Fingering my Rosary in my pocket, I remained staunch in my demand as I replied, "You have to start on the road back to God sooner or later or suffer the ramifications. I am getting out of the service in a few days and I am going to leave knowing that you have squared yourself with God." "But I can't go to Communion," was his weak response. "You can make a spiritual Communion." It was now 10:15 a.m. The Mass would start in fifteen minutes. I continued praying Hail Mary's. He washed up, dressed, and his last feeble defense was, "Can I wait until next Saturday so I can go to Confession?" "No." We were in the car on our way. I knew a spiritual miracle was taking place.

He drank in the beauty of all his surroundings. The trees looked more majestic the shrubs were greener and the blossoms more beautiful. The sky was bluer the air fresher!

The Mass over, we walked to the car and he seemed to have found what he was searching for "He who seeks God has already found Him," said Graham Greene. We shared a lunch at the mess hall consisting of chicken, potatoes, gravy, hot biscuits, corn on the cob, coffee and ice-cream. It was one of the most enjoyable meals I ever shared. During the course of the meal, tactfully, I told him he would no longer live the way he had—Hell would be the consequence!

Three years after my discharge, I received a letter from the Master Sergeant whom this man had contacted and begged to search the records for my address, write me, thanking me, and informing me that he had entered a Monastery! I recalled St. Louis de Montfort's words, "Even if you are on the brink of damnation, even if you have one foot in hell, even if you have sold your soul to the devil . . . The Rosary will obtain contrition and pardon for your sins." Here was a soul on the brink of damnation with one foot in hell!

No wonder that among the myriad forms of Marian devotion which have developed over the centuries in the Church, the Rosary undoubtedly holds pride of price.

"She is the Queen of Heaven and earth, foreshadowed in Divine Wisdom" said St. Nicholas of Flue, telling a friend of Mary's important role.

History proves that St. Nicholas of Flue was instrumental in Switzerland being an independent and united country today. Major cities Lucerne and Zurich, would have drifted into a non-Swiss alliance had it not been for this concerned mystic who grew under the inspiration of Mary whom he held in the highest esteem. Through Her Rosary—which he was never seen without—She had banished the clouds of darkness from his soul, as She was his bridge to God.

It is important to remember that the Rosary is a powerful weapon the Mother of God uses against the forces of evil. In 1951, Pope Pius XII wrote, "We do not hesitate to affirm again publicly that we put great confidence in the Holy Rosary for the healing of evils which affect our times." In 1965, Pope Paul VI wrote the Bishops of the world, "We do not fail to lay stress on the praying of the Rosary, the prayer so dear to Our Lady and so highly recommended by the supreme Pontiffs."

The Rosary (described by food editor of *Redbook* magazine, Bernice Burns) is a familiar sight. It has been used by writers and artists for centuries, and more recently by photographers and movie directors, as a prop signifying prayer. We see a pair of hands, usually worn and wrinkled, clasping a string of beads, and an impression is conveyed. The onlooker may not know what prayers are being said or to whom they are directed, but almost everyone will recognize the Rosary, a string of beads signifying prayer!

Who is She to whom we say the Rosary? Nineteen centuries have not been sufficient to recount the magnificence of Mary. Human as you and I, She became the Daughter of the Father, Bride of the Holy Ghost and Mother of Christ. A girl who walked most humbly on the earth and was crowned the Queen of Heaven. She is Jewish and She is Christian; She is a Virgin and a Mother; She is joyful and full of sorrow. The link that all men see as the answer to the eternal mystery, She is our Mediatrix at the Throne of God, forever.

Why do we pray the rosary? Because Mary has revealed that it is the form of prayer most dear to Her Heart. It is a pledge of faith, a prayer to the Father, a tribute to the Trinity, a salute to Mary and a plea to Her to help us NOW—the only moment important in the eyes of God and at the hour of our death, when we shall await the justice of Her Son.

Where do we pray the Rosary? Anywhere, even the oddest places and times! While walking or driving a car, riding in a bus or waiting for one, while scrubbing the floor or plowing the field, you can pray the Rosary. When you can't sleep, the Rosary will help you forget past troubles and future problems. It is an antenna dotted and dashed with beads which can carry your message to the Queen of Heaven from anywhere in this world.

The August/September, 1987, issue of *Hearts Aflame*, carried an excellent story on the power of Our Lady. Louis Budenz abandoned his Catholic faith as a young man and became the most famous Communist in the U.S.A. He was editor of the Party's national newspaper, the *Daily Worker*.

In 1937, the Party had given orders to ingratiate itself with the Catholic Church. Budenz contacted the best known priest in the country, Fulton Sheen, who was reaching millions of listeners every Sunday with his Catholic hour radio broadcasts.

The two intellectuals discussed Communism and Catholicism for quite a while as they sat at a table in the grill room of the Commodore Hotel on E. 43rd St. in Manhattan. They talked away until finally the Msgr. pushed aside the remaining cutlery on the table, bent forward with his piercing eyes and exclaimed:

> "Let us now talk of the Blessed Virgin!"
>
> "Immediately," wrote Budenz ten years later, "I was conscious of the senselessness and sinfulness of my life as I then lived it. The peace that flows from Mary, and which had been mine in the early days, flashed back to me with an overwhelming vividness.
>
> "There ran in my ears for a moment the prayer which comes from the salutation of Gabriel: *Ave Maria, gratia plena*! 'Hail Mary, full of grace!' How often, I thought, has that supplication gone up from thousands in distress and brought them peace—and I, who know better, reject it. . . .
>
> "The wholeness and holiness of the life I had deserted were laid before me. To regain the peace that is the product of devotion to Mary was still possible. I caught my breath at the prospect; I was quietly laboring under an intense strain."

The conversation, Budenz wrote later, had to do specifically with Lourdes, with the promises of Our Lady of

Fatima, with the prayers of the Church for the conversion of Russia, and Our Lady's power to see them fulfilled. "What stood out in this discussion," said Budenz, was the dignity of the human personality represented by the whole spiritual concept centered in Mary.

Of all the episodes in his long career, Budenz continued, "this memento to Mary was the most electric, the most awe-inspiring . . . never has my soul been swept by love and reverence as it was that April evening."

Budenz went on writing and editing Communist propaganda for the *Daily Worker* for nine more years. Finally, he said what the Msgr. had been praying for and waiting to hear. Budenz said that he wanted to have his wife and three daughters baptized in the catholic Church.

It all started with those eight words after dinner at the Commodore Hotel: "Let us now talk of the Blessed Virgin."

Considered one of the greatest clients of Mary, St. Bernard would preach Her powerful intercession:

> My dear children, She is the ladder by which sinners may ascend to heaven; She is my greatest hope, and the whole ground of my hope. For can the Son repulse Her or be Himself repulsed? Will He refuse to hear, or not be Himself heard?

Along with St. Thérèse the Little Flower, St. Francis Xavier is the patron of the missions. He was distinguished by his tender devotion to the Mother of God. It was on the feast of Her Assumption that he made his first vows. He was accustomed to offer up all his petitions to God through the intercession of Mary; and, in his public instructions, after begging the gift of a lively faith for himself and his listeners, he addressed himself to Mary, Whom, in the conclusion of his talk, always saluted with the "Hail Holy Queen." He undertook nothing without first recommending it to God through Mary. Far from being ashamed of being called Her servant, he gloried in this title, and carried his Rosary around his neck, to manifest it to all. Many of the miracles he was instrumental in performing were done through his Rosary. On being asked for some token by a merchant of Meliapore, India, who was about to embark for Malacca, he gave him his Rosary saying, "They will be of some use to you, provided you have confidence in Mary."

In his instructions, he always insisted much on the greatness of the Mother of God, and spared no exertion to induce others to place themselves under Her protection. At the moment of his death—which occurred on the Island of Sancian, almost in sight of China—he appealed to Our Lady, by often repeating the beautiful and touching language of the Church, "Show Thyself a Mother."

At the close of life, when we are as it were on the threshold of eternity, then, says St. Jerome, Mary not only comes to us when called, but even spontaneously advances to meet us.

St. Francis Borgia's boundless confidence that he had in Jesus, as His Savior and Mediator, was founded principally on Mary, whom he regarded as his advocate with Her Divine Son. He sought to make all men participate in his feeling toward Her, and his confidence in Her intercession. Daily he said special prayers to Her, especially the Rosary.

Peter Richard Kenrick, in his *Month of Mary*, says,

What more efficacious means of promoting the diffusion of Catholic Truth and Catholic piety can be employed, than to accompany all our efforts for both, by carrying about Mary in our hearts, and encouraging others to the practice of this devotion? The Church, solemnly addressing Her, says: "Rejoice, O Virgin Mary, because thou alone hast destroyed all heresies." This was the language of men who had practical experience of its truth. This was the sentiment of those faithful dispensers of God's mysteries, who, both in ancient and modern times not only overcame the attacks made on their own souls, but also made great inroads among God's

enemies, either by bringing whole nations into the fold of
Christ, or by renewing the face of the earth among degener-
ate Christians. If we wish that our exertions should be
crowned by equally glorious results, we must use the same
weapons which rendered them successful. We shall find that
devotion to Mary is the great bulwark of Christian faith and
morality; because it cannot be practiced, without imparting
to those who adopt it a more accurate notion of the Incarnation of the son of God and a more feeling sense of its immense advantages to us than can be otherwise communicated.

The efficacy of Mary's intercession has been experienced and celebrated in all ages of the Church. By means of
it have the most hardened sinners been converted, and, by
the fervor of their penance have consoled the Church, which
they had before scandalized by their conduct. By it has many
a wavering heart been confirmed in its virtue, many a luke-
warm soul roused to practice virtues.

Orators, poets, painters and sculptors—not only in one
age or country—but in every age and country where Christianity has been known have combined to celebrate Her
praises, and transmit to future generations the feelings of religious veneration which they themselves experienced.

Father Faber said:

I cannot conceive a spiritual man who does not habitually
say the rosary. It may be called the Queen of indulgenced
prayers. It consists of the Our Father, Glory Be and the Hail
Mary, whose Authors are Our Blessed Lord Himself, the
Archangel Gabriel, St. Elizabeth, the Council of Ephesus,
and the whole Church.

It is a complete abridgment of the Gospel—expressing
the three great phases of the work of the Redemption; Joy,
Sorrow and Glories of His Mother; yet it is all the ONE Jesus as Mary saw Him, Mary's view of Him, Love of Him,
which the complete Rosary brings to us. It unites mental
with vocal prayer. It is a devotional compendium of theology. It is an efficacious practice of the presence of God. We

should first make a picture of the mystery, and always put the Blessed Lady in the picture, for the rosary is Hers. We should ask for some virtue with each mystery, and fix on some soul in Purgatory to whom to apply the vast indulgences granted to this devotion.

In October of 1987, I brought the International Pilgrim Virgin Statue to the Poor Clares Monastery in Aptos, California. There I was given a Rosary made by Mother Francis. She made it from the volcanic ash that blew when Mt. St. Helen's volcano erupted on May 18, 1980.

The blast was 500 times greater than the 20-kiloton atomic bomb that fell on Hiroshima.

How much more powerful is Our Lady's intercession through the Rosary. She has the power to change hearts and turn them to God, to restore peace on earth and bring God's grace to all humanity.

The Rosary has been one of the greatest safeguards of families in the midst of corruption and evil influences. In all the countries where the Family Rosary is prayed, we see that the Faith is quite strong and that the faith is handed down from one generation to the next.

At Paris, in 1852, the world-renowned Dr. Recamier was dying. He was not only a great doctor and scientist of international fame, but he was also a man of deep faith and piety. Once, at a medical meeting, he surprised his colleagues by appearing with a Rosary hanging from his wrist. What! A man of such learning, a surgeon of such repute, a world famous authority on medical science, the advisor of rulers regarding their health—reciting the Rosary like a little old lady! Noting the general amazement, Recamier calmly declared,

> Yes, gentlemen, that's correct, I do say the rosary. When I see that medical science is powerless in a desperate case, I have recourse, through the intercession of the Mother of God, to Him Who alone can help me. And I must confess,

that I have truly obtained wonderful results. (Thiamer, Simb. d. Ap.)

Let us bravely show to everyone our love for Our Blessed Mother. It would be wonderful if every home would erect an altar with Mary's statue or picture in it. The family could gather in front of the altar and pray the Family Rosary, and pray there at any time they wished, in time of joy or sorrow. May devotion to Mary lead us to the feet of Jesus in the Tabernacle.

Sister Lucia (the living Seer of Our Lady at Fatima) said this in a letter to a Sister in St. Dorothy's Order, September 16, 1970.

> The prayer of the Rosary or five decades of it, after the Holy Liturgy of the Eucharist, is what most unites us with God by the richness of the prayers that compose it. . . .
>
> Moreover, after the Holy Liturgy of the Eucharist, the prayer of the Rosary is what best fosters in our spirit the growth of the mysteries of Faith, Hope and Charity. Without these virtues we cannot be saved. The Rosary is the prayer of the poor and the rich, of the wise and the ignorant. To uproot this devotion from souls is like depriving them of their daily spiritual bread. She is what supports that little flame of faith that has not yet been completely extinguished from many consciences. Even for those souls who pray without meditating, the simple fact of taking the beads to pray is already a remembrance of God, of the supernatural.

If you love Mary, you will definitely grow in holiness in spite of yourself. Mary understands our needs, our quirks, our circumstances. She will sanctify us in any situation if we allow Her to take charge of our life. We can always rely on Her because She has a solution to our every problem. She writes straight with crooked lines! May Mary be a bit of heaven to us already on earth.

Our Blessed, Loving Mother made the following 15 tremendous PROMISES to all Christians who pray the daily

Rosary! They were told to St. Dominic and Blessed Alan de la Roche. These promises are so powerful and profound, that I would advise taking one promise a day and meditating on it.

1. Whoever shall faithfully serve me by the recitation of the Rosary, shall receive signal graces.
2. I promise my special protection and the greatest graces to all those who shall recite the Rosary.
3. The Rosary shall be a powerful armour against hell, it will destroy vice, decrease sin, and defeat heresies.
4. It will cause virtue and good works to flourish; it will obtain for souls the abundant mercy of God; it will withdraw the hearts of men from the love of the world and its vanities, and will lift them to the desire of eternal things. Oh, that souls would sanctify themselves by this means.
5. The soul which recommends itself to me by the recitation of the Rosary, shall not perish.
6. Whoever shall recite the rosary devoutly, applying himself to the consideration of its sacred mysteries shall never be conquered by misfortune. God will not chastise him in His justice, he shall not perish by an unprovided death; if he be just he shall remain the grace of God and become worthy of eternal life.
7. Whoever shall have a true devotion for the Rosary shall not die without the sacraments of the Church.
8. those who are faithful to recite the Rosary shall have during their life and at the death the light of god and the plenitude of His graces; at the moment of death they shall participate in the merits of the saints in paradise.
9. I shall deliver from purgatory those who have been devoted to the Rosary.
10. The faithful children of the Rosary shall merit a high degree of glory in Heaven.
11. You shall obtain all you ask of Me by the recitation of the Rosary.
12. all those who propagate the Holy Rosary shall be aided by Me in their necessities.
13. I have obtained from My Divine Son that all the advocates of the Rosary shall have for intercessors the entire celestial court during their life and at the hour of death.

14. all who recite the Rosary are my sons and daughters, and brothers and sisters of My only Son, Jesus Christ.

15. Devotion of My Rosary is a great sign of predestination.

When Saint Dominic was in the forest praying, weeping, and afflicting himself with harsh penances so as to obtain the conversion of sinners and heretics, Our Lady appeared to him. This is what She said:

> Dear Dominic, do you know which weapon the Blessed Trinity wants to use to reform the world? I want you to know that in this kind of warfare, the battering ram has always been the Hail Mary, which is the foundation stone of the New Testament. Therefore, if you want to reach these hardened souls and win them over to God, preach the Holy Rosary.

Our Lord Himself appeared to St. Dominic and said:

> Before doing anything else, priests should try to kindle a love of prayer in people's hearts and especially a love of the Holy Rosary. If only they would all start saying it and would really persevere, God, in His Mercy, could hardly refuse to give them His grace. So I want you to preach the Holy Rosary.

After St. Dominic died, Blessed Alan de la Roche restored devotion to the Rosary. Our Lady was so grateful to him that she gave him a great privilege: She called him Her "new spouse." As a token of Her chaste love, She gave him a ring for his finger, a necklace made from Her own hair and a beautiful Rosary.

How comforted we should be that in this world engulfed in evil, we have the Rosary as our shield of protection. The Rosary is our Tower of strength against the enemy, the enemy who would like to attack our mind through intellectual pride. Let us continue to pray the Rosary and Our Blessed Mary will lead Her faithful army to victory.

St. Bonaventure hails Her:

O Mary, full thou art, of the unction of mercy,
And of oil, compassionate. The King falls in love
With your beauty—without—But greater—within.

To sum up everything briefly it can be said, If you want
to grow in holiness: love Our Blessed Mother Mary!

Christic or Chaos

*The power thus put in Her hands is all but unlimited.
How unerringly right, then, are Christian souls when they
turn to Mary for help as though impelled by an instinct of
nature, confidently sharing with Her their future hopes
and past achievements, their sorrows and joys, com-
mending themselves like children to the care of a
bountiful Mother. Among Her many other titles we find
Her hailed as "The reparatrix of the whole World."*
(Leo XIII, *Adiutricem Populi*, Sept. 5, 1895)

When a child runs to its mother, it is because that child
wants something. When we go to Our Lady in prayer, it is
because we want something from God. But, when a mother
rushes to her child, it is because that child is in danger. And
when Our Lady rushed to us, her spiritual children, at Fatima, it is because we are in great danger. Into no century
would She march with such alarming urgency as our 20th.
"Like an army in battle array" She announced,

> I am the Lady of the Rosary. I have come to warn the faith-
> ful to amend their lives and to ask pardon for their sins.
> They must not offend Our Lord anymore, for He is already
> too grievously offended by the sins of men. People must say
> the Rosary. Let them continue praying it every day.

And opening Her hands, with 70,000 people present, She
made them reflect the rays of the sun as She rose. Lucia
pointed instinctively to the sun and cried out to the people:
"Look at the sun!"

The sun, taking the form and color of a dark and silvery disc which did not affect the sight, broke through a previously darkened sky, and began to whirl about as it lowered itself, threatening to fall upon the earth. The crowd watching were terrified and begged God's mercy asking pardon for their sins.

As though Our Lady of the Rosary couldn't put enough emphasis on the importance of that powerful prayer, during the ten to fifteen minutes of the miracle of the sun, She displayed, only for the three little children, three separate visions. The first was of St. Joseph and the Child Jesus and Our Lady dressed in white with a blue mantle symbolic of the Joyful Mysteries of the Holy Rosary. The second was of Our Lady of Sorrows symbolic of the Sorrowful Mysteries of the Holy Rosary. The final was of Our Lady dressed in Her brown finery as the Lady of Mt. Carmel, symbolic of the Glorious Mysteries of the Holy Rosary.

For the first time in twenty centuries of apparitions, She marches to us with the Rosary and the Brown Scapular. It is thought provoking to ponder St. Dominic's 13th century prophecy of Our Lady, "One day, through the Rosary and the Scapular, She will save the world."

And never has the world been in such dire need of help. That there is a tremendous crisis wracking and troubling the whole world today, cannot be denied. In *Fatima International*, November 4, 1986, Robert Bergin aptly pin-points the current status of our world,

> All humanity is in travail, crying out for help today, for they have problems of the psyche stemming from their alienation from God. Wealth does not make them happy, nor pleasure, nor power, nor high intellectual attainments.

It is sin that is destroying our world. Money, material possessions, fame and power are supposedly the measurement of a man's success in life—no matter how he attains it.

Our Lady asked us to give up our sins or else, she warned,

> Russia will spread her errors throughout the world, causing
> wars and persecution of the Church. The good will be mar-
> tyred, the Holy Father will have much to suffer, various na-
> tions will be annihilated.

It appears as though we have the choice of giving up
our sinful ways and accepting the chain of the Rosary, or
keeping our sinful ways and accepting the chain of atheistic
communism.

On October 14, 1917, the day after the great miracle of
the sun, the largest newspaper in all of Portugal—and still
the largest today—carried a detailed account of the miracle
of the sun,

> From the height of the road where the people parked their
> carriages and where many hundreds stood, afraid to brave
> the muddy soil, we saw the immense multitude turn towards
> the sun at its highest, free of all clouds. The sun called to
> mind a plate of dull silver. It could be stared at without the
> least effort. It did not burn or blind. It seemed that an
> eclipse was taking place. All of a sudden a tremendous
> shout burst forth, "Miracle, miracle! Marvel, marvel!"

Excluding the Resurrection of Jesus Christ, this is the
only miracle in the history of the world that God would perform that would be predicted time and place in advance.
And it would be so stupendous that the brilliant French
philosopher, Paul Claudel, would describe it as "An explo-
sion of the Supernatural", while the Jesuit scientist, Pio Scia-
tizzi, would refer to it as "The most obvious and colossal miracle in history."

Lucia had begged Our Lady on July 13, 1917, three
months previously,

> I wish to ask You to tell us who You are, and to perform a
> miracle so that everyone will believe that You have ap-

peared to us.

Our Lady replied,

In October I will tell you who I am and what I wish, and will
perform a miracle that everyone will have to believe.

Interestingly enough, in that same apparition Our Lady
stated,

Continue to pray the Rosary every day, in honor of Our
Lady in order to obtain peace for the world and the end of
the war (WWI), because only She can obtain it.

In his marvelous book, *Meet The Witnesses*, John M.
Haffert interviewed thirty three people in 1960 who actually
were present for the great miracle of the sun. Quoting from
his book, here is what several witnesses have said. The first
one, Dona Maria Teresa Charters, twenty-six years of age at
the time, was in the Cova with several relatives. She had
come, she explains, because if something was going to happen, "I wanted to see it with my own eyes".
    "And what did you see?"
    "We distinctly saw the sun, without harm to the eyes.
the sun came down turning on itself, and throwing beams of
several colors."
    "Were you afraid?"
    "I thought we were all to die, but I was not afraid."
    From Augusto Pereira dos Reis, who was also twenty-
six years old, and was standing on the outskirts of the crowd
where the Basilica now stands.
    "I saw the sun doming down, spinning," he explains.
    "Did you experience anything else?"
    "Yes, my clothes were first wet, and then dry."
    "How did you feel when it was over?"
    "I felt more calm."

"Did you know of anyone who did not see it?"

"No."

"And why do you think it happened?"

"In order that we believe more that Our Lady appeared there."

From Antonio Antunes de Oliveira who was thirty-two years old:

"Did you believe that a miracle would take place?"

"At first I did not believe."

"Was it raining very much?"

"Yes, it rained much. I was wet. There was a great deal of mud" . . . .

"What did you see?"

"I looked at the sun. It did not hurt my eyes . . . . There were many people kneeling in the mud, and I was one of them."

"Were you far from the children?"

"Yes, I was far from the children, and could only see them when they were taken up in the arms of some people. One of these people was Joao Machado, who had no faith."

"What else did you see?"

"I looked at the sun and saw it spinning like a disc, rolling on itself. I saw the people changing color. They were stained with the colors of the rainbow. Then the sun seemed to fall down from the sky."

"Were you afraid?"

"I was afraid that the sun would fall down as the people said that the world was going to end."

"Was everyone around you afraid?"

"They were afraid and screaming."

"And what did they say about it?"

"They said it was a miracle."

"What did you think?"

"I thought it was a great miracle."

"Did it affect your life?"

"I now go to Fatima almost every month, and continue to have always the same faith."

Manuel Francisco, a farmer, was twenty-seven years of age and was standing in the crowd with his wife.

"The sun began to come down until it seemed we were almost near it, and it threw beams of light. It was getting dark and all the people screamed."

"How did you feel?"

"I was so afflicted that I came home weeping."

"But what did you do immediately after the miracle?"

"I went to say some prayers close to the spot where the vision appeared, then came home."

"Were you still weeping?"

"My heart was afflicted. I could not help crying."

Mr. Haffert concluded this last interview by asking,

"What kind of event would have caused a strong country farmer of the Serra d'Aire Mountains, head of a family, in the prime of his manhood, to weep?"

The tremendous miracle of the sun completed, WWI ending soon, as Our Lady had said it would, She gave us ample warnings of another more horrible war, WWII! Strange, it seems that WWI came to an end in 1918, in the eleventh month, on the eleventh day—at the eleventh hour. . . .!

She told us in that famous Third apparition,

The War (First World War) is going to end. But, if people do not stop offending God, another more terrible war will begin in the reign of Pope Pius XI. When you see a night illumined by an unknown light, know that this is the great sign given you by God that He is about to punish the world for its crimes, by means of war, famine, and persecutions of the Church and the Holy Father.

Mankind did not repent! The light came. It was seen in many portions of the world, but predominantly in Europe. It was a blood-red, leaping, flaming, fiery light that danced about the skies all night long. In Germany and Austria people stepped out of their homes and stared into the crimson sky with utter amazement. In southern France, people raced around the country-side looking for priests to hear their confessions as they thought it was the end of the world. The *London Times* of that day carried an article which said that occultists were claiming this was an omen that the world would be struck with a great punishment. Off the coast of Belgium, for the first time in memory, commercial fishermen refused to put their ships to sea that day. In Amsterdam, Holland, the suicide rate, averaging 1-1/2 per day, tripled. In Hungary, animals and people were awakened at 3:00 in the morning by the intensity of this light. In Switzerland, at 6:00 p.m. the Swiss Alps are always pitch black. This particular night they were blood red. In Warsaw, Poland, people in hospitals had to be reassured this was not the end of the world. And in Russia, people never left their homes that entire day.

That light appeared on January 25, 1938. In less than two months, Adolph Hitler would trigger off WWII by marching his goose-stepping soldiers into Austria—a war that would see the death of 55,000,000 people as opposed to 10,000,000 in WWI.

Ironically, the night that light appeared is the feast day of the conversion—and that is what Our Lady wants from us, *conversion*—of St. Paul, formerly known as Saul of Tarsus. It too was a blinding light he had seen in the sky that brought about his conversion. The light that Paul saw was Christ. And Christ said, "I am the light of the world." The most haunting saying that came out of WWI was "The lights are going out all over Europe!" Again, Christ is the light of the world.

It appears as though man gives more homage to the queens of this world, than he does to the Queen of Heaven. Yet, never before have we had to give Her homage and pay attention to Her plea. We don't question the authority of the Queen of Spain in the days of Columbus—or her power. When all else failed, Christopher prevailed on the intelligence and influence she had, to acquire ships and provisions for his quest for the New World.

Men and women alike bowed and cringed before the Virgin Queen of England, Elizabeth. She could reward those who won her favor and cruelly punish those who incurred her wrath, deserved or undeserved. No one questioned her rights or her form of justice.

When a king sits on a throne, the queen is awarded the same honor and devotion as the king by virtue of being his wife. No one questions this or says, she isn't the same as the king, she's just a very well known woman. The reason? They know that the queen can complain to the king and perhaps it will be—off with their heads!

If Our Lady had resided in a grand palace with Our Lord, Her Son, it seems certain She would have been praised, honored and even glorified along with Her Son, if He also had lived in a grand manner. She did, however, share His poverty, humility and suffering in the same patience and silence. What better reason for the King of the Universe to reward Her by giving Her an unequaled status in this same universe—Queen of Heaven and Earth, Queen of Angels and of men? Did She not earn a place of honor beside Her beloved Son? Not only a loving Son, but a just Son, could do no less.

Until we become educated in the ways and mind of God, man cannot comprehend what he does not see, hear and experience. To the unenlightened, to elevate a poor, simply attired woman, doing servile work, to the highest place in Heaven seems incomprehensible. But who can know the mind of God? Our ways are not His ways. Until man, through prayer, spiritual reading, meditation, begins to unite his soul with that of God, his finite mind cannot begin to understand the things of God.

Where there is no devotion to Mary, there is very little devotion to God—a disbelief in the divinity of Jesus and, through fear of damnation, a form of worship based on a contract relationship. 'You do this for me and I'll do this for you—and you'd better come through—because your Book says,"Ask and you shall receive, look and you shall find, knock and the door will be opened to you.'

What is the attitude of those who base their whole belief on Scripture (their own interpretation of it) after reading the words of Elizabeth, "And who am I that the Mother of my Lord should come to me?" and again at the marriage at Cana, when Our Lord told His Mother that His time had not yet come, and She answered by saying to the chief steward, "Do whatever He tells you."

That should say more than anything of Her great position. And She still continues to tell us, "Do what He tells you." That's Her great message. Meditation on the words referring to Our Lady has obviously filled volumes—since so many books have been written about them and yet so many don't hear them. It really is a matter of WON'T hear them. It would mean giving up control of their will. And yet, never before, has it been so imperative that we listen to Her. In their book *Toward a Human World Order*, Gerald and Patricia Mische said,

> There is every evidence that the mass exodus from organized religion in our century has not been due primarily to a loss of belief in a spiritual force informing and encompassing all life. A more frequent cause has been the impotency of organized religion in the face of the struggles and crises—both personal and global—that mankind confronted in the twentieth century. What was being demanded of mankind seemed more than could be met within traditional religious structures. Many were taken up in awe of a new supernatural—technology—and its seeming promise of personal fulfillment and human salvation! The hungry would be fed,

the thirsty given drink, the homeless sheltered, the ill made well, the tired laborer given leisure—more by the power of machines than by power of religion. Religion steadily lost its power to affect human behavior or provide meaning.

Nor was it able to provide social cohesion or cultural security in the face of the threats, conflicts and power struggles between nations of the world. People sought security more in the new technology (which would provide for their physical and economic needs) and in the nation-state (which would provide for their physical safety from the "enemy", the "outsider", the "evil ones") than they did in religion.

The more dire the need, in all ages, the closer the faithful gathered about the Blessed Mother of God.

In these days of distress, when modern materialism has pitted its strength against spiritual endeavor, there has to be a sweeping renewal of devotion to Mary. She is the human Mother of Jesus and the supernatural Mother of every Christian. By nature, a mother is one who gives. God made Mary that she may give to others. To give, one must have; to share, one must possess. The saintly priest of France, Father Olier, insists that the Triune God was pleased to enrich Mary with the maximum of His treasures,

> God united and bestowed on Mary all the perfections He had given to all the just souls of the ancient law, so that She alone had more of the spirit of Christ than all the priests, patriarchs, judges, prophets, kings, all the saints of the Old Testament, and all the just of the Gentile nations ever possessed. From the very moment of Mary's conception, the Holy Spirit poured out on Her more graces than all the most perfect and most eminent souls together ever possessed or ever will possess.

Her maternal function is to exercise Her power on the present and future needs of humanity down through the ages. If Jesus, hidden in the womb of Mary, could sanctify John the Baptist in Elizabeth's womb, what about the sanctifying power communicated to His Mother to whom He was bound by the most intimate union?

No one thinks it unusual that St. Thérèse the Little Flower would say,

> I wish to spend my heaven in doing good upon earth. I will let fall a shower of roses upon the earth.

There is certainly no doubt that she has done what she has promised. If this is true of St. Thérèse, how much more so would it be true of the Queen of Heaven? Would it not be unreasonable to imagine that Mary is limited in Her action?

God owes it to Himself to be just, as well as merciful, but Mary is not obliged to temper Her mercy with justice. She is most anxious to come to our aid. The more destitute we are, the more indulgent She is; the less we deserve Her help, the more merciful She proves to be.

St. Bonaventure said:

> How could She but be powerful, She merits the triple title:
> Daughter of God, Mother of God, Spouse of God.

She pleads with the Heart of God and is always heard, but, when pleading with the heart of man, She is often repulsed by a stubborn will.

To defeat the erroneous teachings of his time, St. Clement Hofbauer urged his disciples to strive for a great love of Mary. St. Dominic accepted the challenge of dangerous heresies of the Middle Ages with enthusiastic devotion to Mary as his weapon. The Marian Societies were the shock troops for the Catholic-counter Reformation in the 16th and 17th centuries. To this day, security in the faithful following of Christ is always to be found wherever Marian devotion flourishes.

Our Blessed Mother has not only given the world the

Conqueror over all heresies but, through the influence of devotion to Her, She has with greater intensity broken the onrushing billows of false opinions, dispersed and crushed them, so that they were not able to undermine the truths of the faith. It is no exaggeration when the liturgical office of Marian feasts in an antiphon offers the daring words,

> Rejoice, O Virgin Mary, all heresies thou alone hast annihilated on the whole earth.

The Mother of the Redeemer is also the Mother of all the redeemed. Her primary concern is that God's Holy Will be done at all times. As at Cana She admonished the men, "Do whatever He tells you," so too, for 20 centuries, She has reiterated those words in Her many apparitions.

Following Our Lady's advice we can never go wrong. Nor can we outdo her in generosity. Pope Benedict XV, in a talk on Our Blessed Lady delighted in stating,

> It is the constant belief of the faithful, based on long experience, that no fervent child of Mary will be forsaken at the last. . . .

Pope Pius XII was supportive with,

> A tender devotion to the Most Blessed Mother of God is in the judgment of holy men a sign of predilection to heavenly glory. . . . May She obtain from God that now at last the Church and all mankind may enjoy more peaceful days.

St. John Berchman took for his life's motto:

> If I love Mary, I shall be assured of my eternal salvation.

St. Robert Bellarmine gave vent to his confidence in Mary's power:

Truly, one who finds his way to the clement and loving tenderness of Mary, will find life and salvation. No one who loves and honors the Virgin Mother will ever be abandoned by Her.

That this is tne age—and the need—of Mary, cannot be denied. St. Louis de Montfort did not hesitate to say,

God wishes that Mary be at present more known, more loved, more honored than She has ever been. If Our Lord is not known as He ought to be, it is because Mary is still unknown. It is She who brought the Savior into the world the first time; a second time, in the modern age, She will give Her Son to the World.

Our Lady Herself confirmed St. Louis's statement in Her second apparition at Fatima, telling Lucia,

Jesus wants to use you to make me known and loved. He wants to establish the Devotion to my Immaculate Heart in the World. I promise salvation to those who embrace it and their souls will be loved by God as flowers placed by myself to adorn His throne.

When Pope John XXIII gave us Vatican Council II, he made it possible for our Christian brethren to come to a better understanding of Our Lady as the Mother of the Church. The Calvinist, Max Thurian, in his book, *Mary, Mother of all Christians*, makes it unmistakably clear that the ecumenical movement will be without lasting significance if it does not go beyond the stage of expressions of openness and gestures of amity, if it does not result in concrete steps towards unity of doctrine and of worship and few religious teachings have so separated Christians in the past, and have aroused such antagonisms, as have the theology and the veneration of the Virgin Mary and Her true role in the economy of salvation.

Only a mother can unite a family, only Our Lady can

unite Christianity. She gives us a hint of this unity of Christianity with Her most profound words spoken at Fatima,

> In the end My Immaculate Heart will triumph. Russia will be converted, and a period of peace will be granted to the world.

With Edgar Allen Poe, may we all plead,

> At morn, at noon, at twilight dim,
> Maria, Thou hast heart my hymn.
> In joy and woe, in good and ill,
> Mother of God, be with me still.

It has been said, "God's power is in our hands when we pray the Rosary!" It can do what no other prayer can in todays crises.

John Henry Cardinal Newman said,

> The Blessed Virgin is called powerful, and even all-powerful, because She, more than any other, more than all the angels and saints, has this great prevailing gift of prayer. No one has access to the Almighty in the same way as His Mother. Her Son will never refuse anything She asks of Him, and this is the source of Her power. So long as Mary defends the Church, no power on earth or of the evil spirits, or great Monarchs or human strength, or popular violence (atheistic communism) will be able to harm Her; for human life is short but Mary reigns in Heaven, eternally Queen.

President Ronald Reagan, in 1985, fully understanding the great tension in a world on the verge of WWIII said,

> In the prayers of simple people . . . like the children of Fatima, there resides more power than in all the great armies and statements of the world.

And the practice, by millions upon millions of people, of

praying the daily Rosary is growing tremendously throughout
the world thanks to the Rosaries for Peace Crusade.
Catholics and Protestants stand united through their devotion to Mary in the Rosary. If we are to survive the holo-
causts which threaten us today, countless other millions must
learn the necessity and efficacy of prayers to Our Lady of the
Rosary.

As the veneration of Mary was the soul of the 13th century—and the reason for its phenomenal achievement—let
us imitate these champions of old and swell the ranks of Her
glorious army as She marshalls our allegiance to Her Son's
commands so that together we can triumphantly march into
that longed for, promised, "era of peace."

Bibliography

Alberione, James, SSP. Std., *Glories and Virtues of Mary*, St. Paul Editions, 1982, *Mary Mother and Model*, St. Paul Editions, 1962, *Mary, Queen of Apostles*, St. Paul Editions, 1976

Augustine, Fr., O.F.M. Cap. *Ireland's Loyalty to Mary*, Kerryman Ltd. 1952

Attwater, Donald, *A Dictionary of Mary*, Catholic Book Publ., Co. 1985

Belloc, Hilaire, *Europe and the Faith*, The Paulist Press, 1939

Bradshaw, Robert, *Frank Duff*, Montfort Publications, 1985

Buehrle, Marie Cecilia, *The Eternal Woman*, Bruce Publ. Co., 1954

Burke, Thomas J.M., S. J., *Mary and the Modern Man*, The American Press, 1954

Carroll, Eamon R., O. Carm., *Understanding the Mother of Jesus*, Michael Glazier, Inc., 1979

Daniel-Rops, Henri, *The Book of Mary*, Hawthorne Books Inc., 1960

Dehan, Peter Thomas, O. P., *Eve and Mary*, Herder, 1957

Doherty, Eddie, *Matt Talbot*, Bruce Publishing Co., 1953

Frings, M. J., Rev., *The Excellence of the Rosary*, Wagner, 1912

Gallery, John I., Rev., *Mary vs. Lucifer*, Bruce, 1958

Graef, Hilda, *The Devotion to Our Lady*, edited by Daniel-Rops, Hawthorn, 1963

Haffert, John M., *Meet the Witnesses*, A.M.I., 1961

Kane, John A., *The School of Mary*, St. Anthony Guild Press,

1943

Kenrick, Peter Richard, *Month of Mary*, The Peter Reilly Co., 1895

Lamberty, Manetta, S.C.C., *The Woman In Orbit*, The Lamberty Co., Inc., 1965

Laurentin, René, *Queen of Heaven*, Translated by Gordon Smith, Clonmore and Reynolds Ltd., 1953

Neubert, Emil, S. M., S.T.D., *Life of Union with Mary*, translated by Sylvester P. Juergens, S.M. S.T.D., Bruce Publ. Co., 1959

Palmer, Paul F., S.J., *Mary in the Documents of the Church*, The Newman Press, 1952

Power, Albert, Very Rev., S.J., M.T., *Our Lady's Titles*, Frederick Pustet Co., 1928

Purcell, Mary, *Matt Talbot and His Times*, The Newman Press, 1955

Ripley, Francis J., Rev., *Mary, The Mother of the Church*, Tan Books and Publishers, Inc., 1969

Roberto, D., Hermit of Monte Corona, *The Love of Mary*, Tan Books, 1951

Sharkey, Don, *The Woman Shall Conquer*, Franciscan Marytown Press, 1954

Shaw, J. G., *The Story of the Rosary*, Bruce, 1954

Sitwell, Gerard, O.S.B., *Spiritual Waters of the Middle Ages*, Hawthorn 1961

Suenens, L. J., Msgr., *Mary the Mother of God*, Hawthorn, 1959

Thurian, Max, *Mary, Mother of All Christians*, Herder 1964

Zundel, Maurice *Our Lady of Wisdom* Sheed and Ward, 1944